THE MEN WHO MADE KINGSTON

Endpaper: Architect's drawing of the Aston Webb façade at the Kingston store, exhibited in the Royal Academy in 1936.

The charter granting Bentalls their coat of arms in 1967

THE MEN WHO MADE KINGSTON

A History of Bentalls of Kingston upon Thames
1867–1995

Peter E Firth

BENTALLS plc
Kingston upon Thames
1995

Copyright © Peter E Firth

ISBN 0 9526537 0 2

Printed and bound in Great Britain by
St Edmundsbury Press, Bury St Edmunds, Suffolk

Contents

LIST OF ILLUSTRATIONS		vi
ACKNOWLEDGEMENTS		ix
FOREWORD		xi
Introduction		1
1	'Observe the Address'	
	How it all began	5
2	'The Man Who Made Kingston'	
	The profound influence of Leonard Bentall	21
3	'Bentalls upon Thames'	
	The Bentalls effect on the town of Kinsgston	51
4	'The Big Idea'	
	The nurturing of good staff relations	71
5	'Our Store, Your Store'	
	Caring for the customers	87
6	'Branching Out'	
	The build-up of branch stores	121
7	'The Planning Application of the Century' – I	
	The gradual accumulation of land and property	137
	'The Planning Application of the Century' – II	
	The concept and development of the Bentall Centre	145
8	'A Store for All Seasons'	
	The family influence and the management of Bentalls	155
INDEX		168

Illustrations

1	Benthall Hall in Shropshire	6
2	Anthony Bentall's shop in Maldon	7
3	Frank Bentall's first advertisement	11
4	The first entries in Frank Bentall's ledger	13
5	Frank Bentall	15
6	No 31 Clarence Street	17
7	The corner of Clarence Street and Wood Street c. 1900	18
8	One of Bentall's first horse-drawn vans	24
9	Part of the Great Potato Queue	27
10	The Clarence Street/Wood Street corner prior to rebuilding	29
11	Leonard Bentall's private office	30
12	Bentalls' electricity generating plant	31
13	The Hermon Cawthra murals	33
14	The opening of Richmond Park golf course	44
15	Leonard Bentall's letter to Sir Charles Lidbury	46
16	Leonard Bentall	48
17	Book signing by the Bedser twins	55
18	Book signing by Joan Collins	58
19	Friendly Finland Fortnight	63
20	Tribute by the Mayor of Kingston	70
21	Fancy dress ball at Clarence House	73

	Illustrations continued	Chapter
22	'Clarencia'	74
23	The 323 (Surrey) Anti-Aircraft Company	78
24	Clarence House river party	82
25	The millinery department c. 1929	88
26	Fleet of delivery vans	94–5
27	The escalator hall	97
28	The Packeteria	98
29	HRH the Queen at the Nylons Shop in 1955	106
30	HRH Queen Mary visiting the store in 1951	107
31	Italy in Kingston window display	109
32	Pat Moss, Mike Hawthorn and Roy Salvadori at Italy in Kingston	111
33	Poster for Italia Romantica	112
34	Michelangelo's David and fig leaf	113
35	The new multi-storey car park	115
36	The Worthing store	124
37	The Ealing store	126
38	Opening of the Bracknell store	130
39	Map showing the locations of the Bentalls stores	135
40	Plan of the Kingston site illustrating 125 years of land acquisition	138–9
41	Wood Street in 1886	141
42	The Aston Webb façade c. 1960	148
43	Gerald Bentall	156
44	Rowan Bentall	156
45	James Spooner	161
46	Edward Bentall	161
47	'The Men Who Made Kingston'	167

Illustrations continued

Colour Plates

Frontispiece
1 *Charter granting the company's coat of arms*

Colour Plates appearing between pages 110 and 111
2 *Watercolour of the depository*
3 *The Bentall Centre during construction*
4 *HM the Queen visiting Kingston in 1992*
5 *Interior of the Kingston store*
6 *Exterior of the Bentall Centre*
7 *Interior of the Bentall Centre*
8 *The Bentalls Board*
9 *Interior of the Bracknell store*
10 *Frontage of the Lakeside store*
11 *Interior of the Tonbridge store*
12 *Statue of Leonard Bentall*

Acknowledgements

I am indebted to a number of people for their help with this book. First and foremost, to the present Chairman, Edward Bentall, fifth in the line of Bentalls to head the company, for his confidence in commissioning the history and his unwavering enthusiasm for the project; to his colleagues on the Board – Grenville Peacock, John Ryan and Tony Anstee – for their invaluable contributions; to Mrs Kate Bentall, widow of the late Rowan Bentall, for permission to use material from *My Store of Memories*, his highly entertaining history of the company up to 1974; to David Fowler, with whom I enjoyed a most agreeable professional association in the production of the *Bentalls Bulletin* prior to his retirement from the Bentalls Board in 1990, for gallantly taking on the job of reading the manuscript for howlers and for his shrewd observations on the text in general; to Mrs Angela Adam, secretary to Edward Bentall, for being so extremely helpful; to Miss Julie Brown for her cheerfulness in the face of endless requests for archive material of which there is, literally, *tons* stored away under her meticulous care; to Roger Whipp of Bentalls' Book Department, Cedric Parkin of the Planning Department, Judy Cake of the Training Department and Keith Solomon and his staff at Hardman Road for their ready cooperation; to Sir Colin

THE MEN WHO MADE KINGSTON

Chandler for an up-date on the Friendly Finland Fortnight; to my friend Barry Shaw for giving me the benefit of his considerable experience of book publishing; to my staff, especially my secretary, Gill McDonnell, for typing and re-typing the manuscript what must have seemed like a hundred times (thank goodness for word processors); to our designer, Sandy Field, for a stunning dust jacket; and finally – and particularly – to my colleague and daughter Louise, who did all the hard work of researching and indexing and generally making my part of the job a breeze.

Foreword

The decision to publish a new history of Bentalls is particularly pleasing for me, since it represents a major part of the history of my family. But it is rather more than that; indeed it would not be stretching a point too far to say that it is in part a history of the life of Kingston over the past century and a quarter.

Since the earliest days of the business, the fortunes of Bentalls have been closely linked with the Royal Borough. The contribution Bentalls have made to Kingston over the past 128 years in terms of revenue from rates alone has been substantial. Needless to say, it has not stopped there. We have contributed to the architectural as well as the social well-being of the town and taken the keenest interest in its planning and development. Since the 1950s we have been active in urging for better access roads and parking facilities, to which end our own multi-storey car park was an important contribution. It was our initiative which led to a study of proposals to build a second crossing of the Thames which would have been an immense boon to the town then – and even more so now that the existing bridge is in need of major repair.

There are three reasons why it was considered timely to publish this history now. The first is that my father's book,

THE MEN WHO MADE KINGSTON

My Store of Memories, written in 1974, is well out of date. The second is that Bentalls recently celebrated our 125th anniversary. The third is that our most important development of the past decade, the Bentall Centre, is now almost fully let. An appropriate moment, then, to pause and take stock as we move forward once more into the future.

Its publication is a tribute to the four generations of Bentalls who laid the foundations of the business as it is today; to my colleagues on the board, including our non-executive directors, for working towards our continuing success; to all our staff, past and present, whose immense loyalty has been one of our greatest strengths; to our suppliers in this country and abroad; and, above all, to our customers, many of whom have been coming to Bentalls for generations, without whom our efforts would have been for nothing.

L Edward Bentall
Kingston upon Thames
Autumn, 1995

Introduction

It has been described as Greater London's greatest store. Outside London, it is the best known department store in the UK and the 13th largest in Europe. Over the years (the 125th anniversary was celebrated in 1992), Bentalls of Kingston have furnished generations of families in the South East with practically all their needs, from food to furniture, fine wines to fashions, motor cars to cushions, books to bedding, shoes to spectacles, foreign travel to theatre tickets, icing sugar to insurance, perfume to – in one celebrated example of 'customer care' – potatoes. Customers have come to Bentalls to furnish their homes, to put food on their tables, to have their houses bought and sold, or even built for them, and their furniture removed or stored. Whilst in the the store they've been able to have their hair dressed, their photographs taken, their books signed, their letters posted and – an abiding memory of Bentalls for many – to visit Santa in his grotto.

Typical of the close relationship Bentalls have long enjoyed with their customers is the story of the lady who came in to say that her neighbour's bees had swarmed into her garden and, since she *always* went to Bentalls for everything, she *knew* they'd have the answer. In the event, they did. A perplexed sales assistant finally referred the matter to the highest authority; the then Chairman, the late Rowan Bentall, interrupted a Board meeting to come down and reassure the customer that in his experience (fortuitously, his mother had kept bees whilst he was a boy) they would soon move on to a more permanent residence.

How Bentalls attracted and then retained such loyalty is to a large extent the story of this book. It is a story of innovations far ahead of their time, like the installation, against much opposition, of Bentalls' own electricity generating plant which helped to keep not only the store but also the hospitals of Kingston going during the power cuts of the time; of farsighted land acquisitions which have seen the transformation of the site to a degree Frank Bentall when he opened his small draper's shop in 1867 could not have dreamed possible; of imaginative sales promotions one of which contributed to the sale of £128-million worth of British aircraft to Finland; of public service and help for others; and of consideration for staff that has repaid itself a thousand fold, promoting that spirit of service described over a century earlier by the famous historian Edward Gibbon (himself an old boy of Kingston Grammar School) as 'that public virtue' necessary to the health of any society, be it business or empire.

When Ladybird Books Ltd, publishers of that admirable series of 'easy reading' books for children, decided in 1973 to add to their People at Work range a book about life in a big store, Bentalls was the store they chose on which to base it. And when, in 1938, Dinky Toys introduced a new range it included a delivery van in the yellow and green livery of the Kingston store. Only 200 were made. The lone survivor was sold at Christies in 1994 for a world record price for a Dinky model of £12,650, the price of a full-size van. Alas, the buyer was not Bentalls but a French engineer.

One of Bentalls' most remarkable achievements has been the

Introduction

creation of a new store and shopping centre on a four-and-a-half acre site that was acquired not, as most are, as a single strip of land ripe for development but was put together, a piece here, a piece there, like a giant jigsaw puzzle, over a period of 125 years. How some of the pieces were acquired is one of the fascinations of the Bentall story.

Many of the pages of the story carry the indelible imprint of the larger than life figure of Leonard Bentall, son of the founder and man of energy, vision and determination. He more than any other individual shaped the destiny of the company from its 20th year when he joined it, until today, half a century after his death. His was the concept of the Super Store that the Bentalls of today represents. He it was, whilst others shrank back in the dark days of the depression, who embarked on a massive rebuilding programme. It resulted in the celebrated Aston Webb structure recalling the architecture of nearby Hampton Court Palace, the façade of which the Bentall Centre of 1992 retains. Leonard Bentall, shrewd businessman and expansive innovator, autocratic yet progressive employer, benefactor to the town and the trade who once made the time to travel 6,000 miles fund raising for charity, epitomises the philosophy of this unique and most progressive of businesses. Hardly surprising, then, that after his death he should be described by the Mayor of the Royal Borough as 'The man who made Kingston'.

Like many who have weathered the recession of the early 1990s, Bentalls today are leaner than they were in Leonard Bentall's time. Where once he employed 3,500 in his one store, Bentalls now run Kingston and five satellite stores within a 40 mile radius with less than a third of that number of staff. Arguably, it is a fitter business, which only three times in the past two decades has failed to raise its annual turnover above that of the preceding year (from £11 million in 1964 to £84.4- million in

1995). There is still a Bentall at the helm, the present Chairman, Edward Bentall, being a great grandson of the founder. And the spirit of progress personified by Leonard Bentall flourishes in the recent flowering of the 600,000 square foot Bentall Centre, spectacularly combining department store with shopping centre in the biggest development in Bentalls' history and concluding the latest chapter in the story of this store for all seasons.

1. 'Observe the Address'

HOW IT ALL BEGAN

Most of the credit for founding Bentalls of Kingston belongs to Frank Bentall. Most, but not quite all, since a small share should go to the young lady who was to become his wife, Laura Downman. For without the imperative to demonstrate his credentials as a suitor to Laura's sceptical father, Frank might have soldiered on in his father's draper's shop at Maldon in Essex.

There had been a Bentall in the drapery business for at least a generation before Frank. Their ancestors had been landowners and farmers for centuries, tracing their antecedents back to Anfrid de Benetala who appears to have come to England with William the Conqueror in 1066 and to have settled in Shropshire. A manor house built on the estate six centuries later still stands; Benthall Hall, near Much Wenlock, is now run by the National Trust. Its first incumbent was William Benthall, two of whose sons moved from Shropshire to the south east, establishing the Essex branch of the family.

Against the family inclination towards farming, Josiah Bentall, Frank's great uncle, had opened a draper's shop at Maldon in the mid 1800s. In the event Josiah did not remain a

Family Seat: Benthall Hall near Much Wenlock in Shropshire, now run by the National Trust (© The National Trust)

draper for long, returning to farming and disposing of his shop to his cousin Anthony Bentall, Frank's father. Anthony was born in 1811 in nearby Rayne. He, too, decided against a career in agriculture in favour of drapery and, at the time he accepted his cousin's offer, owned a shop in Great Missenden, Buckinghamshire, which he gave up to return to Maldon. It was there that Frank was born in 1843. The Maldon of the day had a strong Nonconformist community and the Bentalls were devout members of the Congregational Chapel. In time, young Frank joined his father in the business with its growing agricultural clientele, many of them close or distant relatives. Following his father's example, Frank then left Essex to broaden his experience. He became apprenticed to a silk mercer in Southampton.

'Observe the Address' Chapter 1

Photograph, dated 1888, of the draper's shop in Maldon, Essex, run by Frank Bentall's father

He took with him to Southampton his commitment to the Congregational church and became a Sunday School teacher. One of his fellow teachers was his bride to be, Laura Downman. She came from a very different background. Her father was a pharmacist in Southampton and regarded his prospective son-in-law with the aloofness which the Victorian middle classes reserved for those engaged in 'trade'. Frank was undeterred. When in 1867 he learned that one James Hatt was offering for sale his small draper's shop at No 31 Clarence Street, Kingston Upon Thames, in Surrey, he saw this as his opportunity to secure Laura's hand and his own business into the bargain.

The asking price for the shop, measuring some 24ft by 40ft, would have been several hundred thousand pounds in today's money. A shop of the same size in Clarence Street today would fetch about £3-million – but that, of course, is long after

Bentalls helped make it Kingston's most fashionable thoroughfare. Even so, the outlay would have been a tall order for an apprentice, so Frank's father lent a helping hand. For all that, the move was not for the faint hearted. Although Surrey's second largest town at the time, Kingston then had a population of only 16,000 inhabitants and no fewer than 25 drapers to serve them. These were the days when drapery was big business, partly to satisfy the Victorians' penchant for crinolines and voluminous petticoats. There had been a bonus for the drapery trade in 1851 in the abolition of the Window Tax, leading to the introduction of plate glass and the consequent upsurge in the demand for lace curtains. Drapery was one of the four cornerstones of Kingston's trade and had been for 300 years. The Four Companies of Kingston, whose constitution was drawn up by Lord Howard of Effingham, High Steward of the Borough, as long ago as 1579, comprised the mercers, butchers, shoemakers and woollen drapers, the last mentioned including fullers, tailors and weavers as well as drapers. On one of the columns in Kingston Parish Church may still be seen the faded remains of a painting of the patron saint of woollen drapers, St Blaize. It was done in the 14th or 15th century and restored in the 19th and shows the saint, the former Bishop of Sebaste in Armenia, carrying a wool comb.

Despite its royal antecedents, being the place where seven Anglo Saxon kings were crowned, Kingston had fallen on hard times. Recently opened was a workhouse for over 300 poor souls and one in 17 of the population were listed as paupers. Of the working population many were farm labourers, who were severely affected by a series of harsh winters when for weeks the ground was unworkable. When the Thames froze over in 1895 local traders – Frank Bentall almost certainly among them – together combined to provide bread and soup, as a poem of the day commemorates.

'Observe the Address' Chapter 1

> *'From the Dolphin to the Clarence good sportsmen formed a ring.*
> *Captain Harvey, Phillips, Fricker, George Campbell and young King.*
> *The Captain then suggested that five hundred quarts or more*
> *Of soup should be distributed amongst our starving poor.*
> *George Campbell, full of mischief – though a pardonable sin –*
> *When Phillips was not looking threw two legs of mutton in.*
> *While Kingston Corporation took small notice of their poor*
> *A few warm-hearted tradesmen brought the fact home to their door.'*

Note: Posterity does not record whether this same George Campbell went on to make soup for the millions, but it's a nice thought . . .

Roads and footpaths were poorly made and maintained and lighting was by gas. To save money, Kingston Gas Company left the lamps unlit when there was a full moon at certain times of the year. In those days traders lived 'over the shop' to be near enough to cope with the exceptionally long opening hours which then and for many years to come were typical of the trade.

Neighbouring shops to Frank Bentall in Clarence Street included a refreshment contractor and restaurateur who specialised in catering for houseboats and other craft on the Thames; a cheesemonger and butter man; a home made jam and marmalade maker; a court, military and naval tailor; and a firm of ironmongers and gunsmiths occasionally patronised by Queen Victoria. Immediately next door to No 31 was the Clarence Arms. Round the corner in Wood Street, itself no more than a muddy lane, was another public house, the Dolphin. Nearby was the Red Lion, two schools belonging to Kingston Parish Church which catered for 750 boys and girls from infants upwards, the Mission House, a pork butcher, two private houses, a clothing shop, a general store for small wares, then the half timbered facade of Kingston vicarage and its one-and-a-half acre walled garden. Opposite was a group of Elizabethan buildings used to house troops in Cromwell's time known then, as now, as the Horsefair, from the name of the street which ran from Wood Street behind the Dolphin.

Frank Bentall's timing in acquiring the business was as fortuitous as James Hatt's was unfortunate. Hatt had been running his draper's business in Clarence Street for nearly 30 years when ill health obliged him to give up at the age of 50. By the standards of the time, this being a year or two before the introduction of public transport in the form of horse drawn trams and before bicycles became commonplace, the location of No 31 Clarence Street was not ideal. Clarence Street was backed by open fields and was on the edge of the town of which the market place, several hundred yards away, was the centre. Its singular advantage was that it was on the main road to Kingston's bridge. As a result, it was destined years later to become the town's main thoroughfare. It took its name from the Duchess of Clarence, later Queen Adelaide, who opened the 'new' Kingston bridge in 1828. The stone bridge, which features in one of the later chapters of this history, replaced a wooden structure dating back to 1200. Although the new bridge was opened a good few years before James Hatt was obliged to sell up, its commercial importance dated from some time later.

Not far north of Clarence Street was Kingston railway station, opened in 1863 – once again, too late for James Hatt to reap the rewards of increased trade. The arrival of the railway in Kingston had been delayed, partly because of vacillation on the part of the Council (not for the only time in this narrative . . .) but mainly because of fears of the impact it was going to have on Kingston's extensive river and coaching trades. It was to be their death knell. Thirty years earlier, the London and Southampton Railway Company had sought permission to run their new line through the town. The request

'Observe the Address' Chapter 1

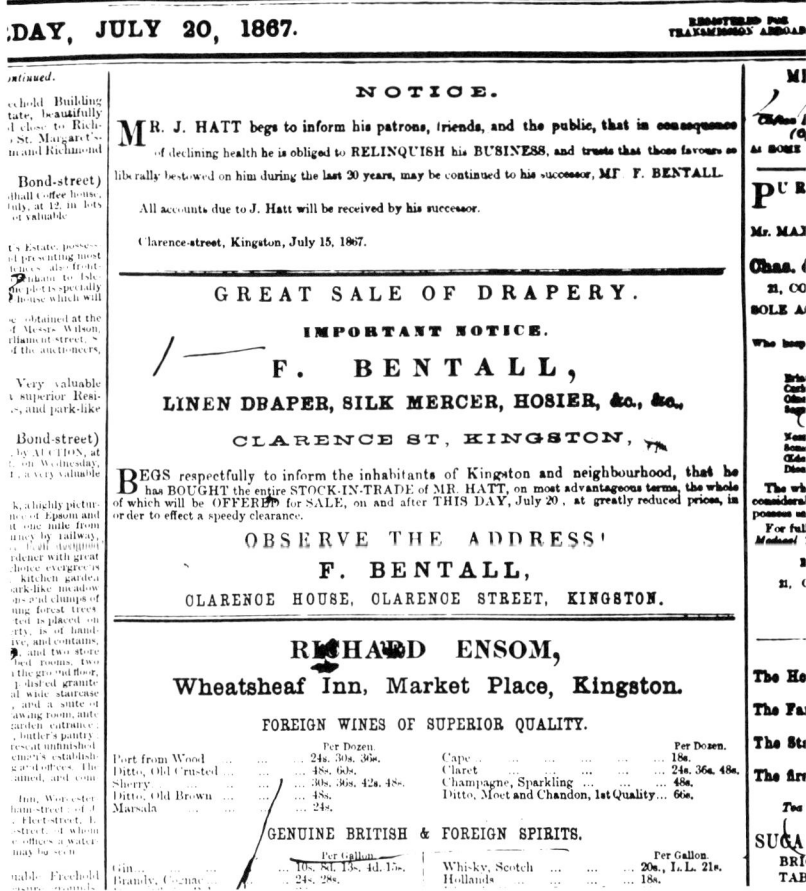

The original advertisement announcing the takeover of James Hatt's business and the beginnings of the Bentalls empire, inserted in the 'Surrey Comet' on 20 July, 1867

was refused by the Council and the line was diverted and the station sited, to Kingston's chagrin, at Surbiton. Surbiton was then no more than a remote corner of the town and called Town End, but soon claimed for itself the unofficial titles of Kingston on Railway and later New Kingston. Kingston

11

Council reacted at last, albeit on the coat tails of a new branch line from Twickenham, and the new station was built. The problem was that the branch line from Twickenham to London was circuitous and slow. However, in 1869 a new and more direct line to the capital was opened via New Malden, Norbiton and Wimbledon which was routed through Kingston. It put the town back on the map.

It was on 20 July, 1867, that Frank Bentall opened his shop. He did so with what can now be described as a characteristically Bentallian flourish, having advertised the event in the *Surrey Comet*, then as now the main weekly newspaper circulating in the town (it had moved from Surbiton, where it was founded in 1854, to Clarence Street in Kingston just four years before Frank Bentall) in the following fashion:

> GREAT SALE OF DRAPERY.
> IMPORTANT NOTICE,
> F. BENTALL,
> LINEN DRAPER, SILK MERCER, HOSIER &c, &c,
> CLARENCE STREET, KINGSTON,
>
> Begs respectfully to inform the inhabitants of Kingston and neighbourhood that he has BOUGHT the entire STOCK-IN-TRADE of MR. HATT on most advantageous terms, the whole of which will be OFFERED for SALE on and after THIS DAY, July 20, at greatly reduced prices, in order to effect a speedy clearance.
>
> OBSERVE THE ADDRESS:
> F. BENTALL,
> CLARENCE HOUSE, CLARENCE STREET,
> KINGSTON

The first entries in Frank Bentall's ledger in his own neat hand showing his first day's takings of £41 2s 6d

Takings on that first day according to Frank Bentall's neatly kept first ledger were £41 2s 6d and, for the week in which the sale continued, £188 4s 8d. This level was not sustained in normal trading in the early days, averaging only £70 a week. However it had increased within a year to £200, on the strength of which Frank had secured the hand of Laura Downman. They were married at Southampton Congregational Church in May, 1868. From the first Frank practised the virtues of personal service and established the foundations on which Bentalls' reputation still rests. Always immaculately dressed, courteous and friendly, he spent almost the whole of his time in the shop, not dealing with the accounts or ordering, which he did after the shop had closed, but serving the customers. At the same time he established another cornerstone of Bentalls' success – excellent relations with his staff. By example, and despite (perhaps because of) the fact that he insisted on the very highest standards of service, down to the meticulous wrapping and tying of parcels, he secured their loyalty and their attentiveness to the needs of those whom they were serving, traditional virtues still cherished by the Bentalls of the 1990s.

We get a glimpse of Frank Bentall, the business and family man, from a brief extract written years later by one of his two sons: 'When I came home from school for my holidays, I used to look with positive awe on my father as a kind of ship which was always carrying full sail. Another thing which struck me about him was that he always seemed to be deliberately laying himself out to set us an example; and later on, when I came to know him in business, there was just the same characteristic especially in little details. Quite unconsciously we boys copied him, and when I was in the business I noticed that others did the same. I do not mean that my father was a 'driver' – but he certainly was out to get things done when they ought to be, and above all as they ought to be. He was impatient of shiftless-

'Observe the Address' Chapter 1

Frank Bentall, who founded Bentalls in 1867

ness and dilatoriness, and had an abhorrence both in home and in business life of any approach to vulgarity in word or voice or deed. I remember him as very dignified, very determined, and always aiming at the most refined form of speech and manner. So much so that I distinctly recall being very harshly punished when I blurted out some vulgar word, which I had quite unwittingly picked up, but which he resented almost as a crime.

'Of course our home life owed a great deal to the quiet tenderness and sympathy of our mother. In every sense she oiled the wheels for us youngsters. My early recollections are chiefly confined to the jolly life I spent at school, and the atmosphere of comfort and dignity at home, and the sense which deepened as the years went by, that it was all obtained by the terribly hard work of my father in his Kingston business.'

Frank and Laura had four children, Alice Emma, George Anthony, Leonard Hugh and Mabel Laura. When both sons joined their father, George in the late 1880s and Leonard in 1893, Bentalls became a family business. The latter, who at one time had aspirations to become an engineer, worked in the Clarence Street shop briefly on leaving school then left, as his father and grandfather had done before him, to gain experience elsewhere, before returning. In Leonard's case this entailed two years as an 'improver' – one step removed from an apprentice – at a store in Peckham and a third year with Peter Jones in King's Road, Chelsea, after which he returned to Kingston.

Bentalls had been established for nearly 30 years when Leonard returned after three years in Peckham and London to join his father and brother and things had moved on, in the town as well as in Bentalls. In three decades the population of Kingston had escalated from 16,000 to 40,000. To accommodate the increase, countless terraces of small houses which give many parts of Kingston their character today, were constructed, as

'Observe the Address' Chapter 1

The shop that spawned a department store – No 31 Clarence Street

was the infrastructure to meet their educational, medical and recreational needs – a technical institute, a hospital, swimming baths and a park, not to mention the installation of electricity and the laying of telephone lines. Bentalls had expanded, too, to a staff of 12 and had built up a business which was steady if not spectacular. Given that many of their customers were earning no more than £1 a week on which they had to feed and clothe their invariably large families, this was not surprising.

It is not difficult against this background to imagine the debates between conservative father and progressive younger son on the future course of the business. In terms of physical expansion, Frank's progress had been cautious. Within a year or so of opening the business he had acquired a small strip of garden next door which he covered in to create a millinery

Clarence Street in 1905

room. Ten years later he acquired the shop next door and that, for the next two decades, was the extent of the Bentalls enterprise. So there is no doubting the influence of young Leonard behind the announcement in May, 1900, four years after he had returned to Kingston, that Bentalls had acquired No 27 Clarence Street, formerly Crossfield's boot shop, and less than six months later No 25, Lewis's confectionery shop, which had one window on Clarence Street and another on Wood Street. As Rowan Bentall wittily observed in *My Store of Memories*: 'Bentalls had turned the corner in more ways than one'.

Ostensibly, the acquisition of Nos 25 and 27 Clarence Street a few years after Leonard had rejoined the business spelt the limit of physical expansion for Bentalls. The properties now adjoining or nearby included several apparently immovable institutions – church school, mission house, vicarage and two pubs. But Leonard's burning ambition, fuelled by his father's motto that 'there's no such word as can't', found a way as ingenious as it was audacious. Only two years after the additions of Nos 25 and 27, he made an offer for the church schools which entailed re-housing the latter in purpose built premises nearby. It was accepted. It enabled the store to expand significantly in depth and, after a major rebuilding exercise, the new Bentalls opened in 1904. But it was no longer a shop. It was the beginning of Bentalls, the department store.

2. *'The Man Who Made Kingston'*

THE PROFOUND INFLUENCE OF LEONARD BENTALL

In 1909, 42 years after founding the business and at the age of 66, Frank Bentall decided to retire. The store had already expanded to a degree he, let alone his father when he helped him buy 31 Clarence Street, could hardly have imagined. It had grown from a small shop of 9,600 sq ft with an annual turnover of £3,600 to a department store extending to three floors and a turnover of £60,000. Yet the next generation was to see even this expansion pale into insignificance.

It was the younger son, Leonard, not George, who succeeded their father as head of the business. Of George comparatively little is recorded, save that he was responsible for buying the store's drapery lines – a key role. One may suppose father and elder son busied themselves with the day-to-day running of the store while the meteor in their midst took off.

What was the make up of this man who was destined to shape Bentalls more significantly than any other person in its 125 year history? Frank, his father, although the family remembered him as a kindly man, was clearly a perfectionist in business and no doubt in family life as well, and his commitment to the church continued throughout his life; he and Laura and the children having moved to Surbiton, he became Sunday School superintendent at the local Congregational church, a post he held for 25 years, long after the family had removed to the more fashionable area of Streatham Park. Leonard's upbringing would undoubtedly have been strict, though not strict enough to diminish a tenacious spirit which as early as his preparatory school days earned him the nickname 'Tiger'.

A life-long love of sport was born during Leonard's boarding school years at New College, Eastbourne; indeed, so enthusiastically did he embrace the school's sporting activities that his father removed him during his final school years to Forest House, then at Woodford, to polish up his academic studies. It was there, too, that he acquired an interest in engineering, to the point of considering making it his career. Fortunately for Kingston, the pull of the family business proved the stronger.

Leonard had spent three years learning the rudiments of the trade before he joined the family business in 1893 and had been there about 16 years when, at the age of 34, he succeeded his father. By that time, due very largely to his influence, it had expanded to include most of the Clarence Street frontage and a good deal behind as well, and had a staff of more than 100. Most of them lived over the shop in accommodation which included a spacious dining hall, reading and other recreational rooms.

The store was already being compared favourably with similar establishments in London's West End in its design and furnishing and its 'offering' of merchandise had by now increased substantially to include departments for hosiery, haberdashery, millinery, boots and shoes, carpets, soft furnishings, dressmaking, ladies' fashions (the Mantle and Costume departments as they were known at the time), in addition to the receiving and dispatch departments in the basement. What's more, it had its own internal telephone system, hand lifts, speaking tubes and electric lighting.

Bentalls' policy for competitive pricing was well established by that date, born no doubt of the necessity to keep prices down in order to trade successfully in a less than affluent area. Leonard spelled out the company's philosophy in a newspaper interview* at the time of the opening. 'We buy everything for cash and therefore we get special discounts and are able to supply goods at particularly low figures but we must have cash payments to carry on such trade. I would like to print in red letters all over your paper that we conduct trade on cash principles only'.

But there was more. Leonard Bentall was one of the first retailers in the UK to guarantee a replacement or a cash refund on any item which proved unsatisfactory. It was a concept he imported from the USA, a frequent source of inspiration to Bentalls thereafter until the present day. His next stroke was to establish a fleet of horse drawn vans in order to provide a free delivery service to all customers living within a 20 mile radius of the store. Free home delivery was to become commonplace in later years, but Bentalls are believed to be the first to have provided it in Surrey.

He began exercising his flair for 'special promotions' at about the same time, starting modestly enough with a window display competition among the staff, judged by the customers. It had all the ingredients of a classic marketing exercise – staff participation, customer involvement and a high profile end product. It was the model on which countless subsequent promotions by Bentalls were based.

Sound business principles were also at work. Hand in glove with the beginnings of a new marketing philosophy was the

---

* *Surrey Comet*, 4 May 1904

One of Bentalls' fleet of horse-drawn vans

ongoing expansion policy, with further additions in 1906. This time there was a difference. The two shops now acquired, Nos 39 and 41 Clarence Street, were not adjoining but were some distance away and separated from Bentalls by several other properties including the Clarence Arms. But negotiations with a neighbouring brewery and a mineral water manufacturer led to the acquisition of pieces of land which together formed a passageway linking Nos 39 and 41 with the store. Leonard's grand design was taking shape.

By now Bentalls were advertising themselves as 'the finest store and shopping centre in Surrey' and had added a number of new departments, for items such as china and glass, toilet ware, silver and electro-plate, stationery, toys and games, leather goods, luggage. But the range and variety of merchandise were not the only attractions. Bentalls had taken to promoting the store by means of extensive local newspaper advertising, through which customers were encouraged to visit the store not just to spend their money but to see the 'beautiful fittings and decoration throughout', 'the great revolution in electric lighting – turning night into day', and the first installation of a pneumatic cash system by the Lamson Tube Company, which was a spectacle in its own right. The Lamson tube system enabled assistants to send cash via brass tubes to a central cash department along a network of wires and tubes fixed to the ceiling rather like an aerial model railway, a guaranteed incentive to encourage small boys to accompany their mother on shopping expeditions.

Bentalls had other ways of encouraging youngsters into the store and for the Christmas trade that same year, 1906, there was a mechanical monkey house, an Old Woman and her Shoe and a tableau of Kingston history, the forerunner of the Christmas grottoes for which Bentalls were to become famous throughout the South East.

At about this time an important appointment was made – the first in what was to become a series from organisations which had much to offer Bentalls – that of Mail Order and Publicity Manager, the man chosen being Herbert H Perkins, from Harrods. Within a year Bentalls had produced their first mail order brochure, numbering 350 pages. In the same year, 1910, another notable 'first' was introduced in the store, the All British Show, a week long promotion which was the inspiration for countless similar events featuring different countries or different types of merchandise almost every year since.

To what extent they were inspired by Herbert Perkins or by Leonard Bentall is not known but there can be little doubt that the Publicity Manager had the full backing of the General Manager. It's thought to have been at his instigation that the store's telephone number was changed to Kingston 1. Herbert Perkins was credited with another significant development in

1912, the change in the name of the business from Frank Bentall to Bentalls. As a third party and someone outside the family he was perhaps best placed to suggest and engineer the move and to assuage the founder's initial resistance to the change with the necessary tact and diplomacy. Leonard, meanwhile, had other concerns, among them improving conditions for his staff and acquiring more premises for yet further expansion. Then, in the midst of all this, came the First World War and with it The Great Potato Sale.

The outbreak of war in 1914 put a temporary stop to Leonard's expansion plans but it was still a busy period for the store, which supplied clothes to the British Army as well as for Belgian refugees. Then, towards the end of the war, Britain faced a potato shortage. Although the Government fixed a retail price for them of one penny three farthings per pound, many wholesalers and retailers disregarded the fixed price and sold at a premium to those who could afford them. Staff employed at Bentalls were among the many who could not. In an act of altruism which was to win him gratitude and not a few new customers, Leonard drove to Norfolk and negotiated the purchase of large quantities direct from the growers. He then offered them for sale at the fixed price of 1¾d – the price at which he bought them – not only to staff but to the general public. Bentalls vans were used to transport the 12,000lbs of potatoes from Norfolk to the store, Bentalls footing the bill.

The great potato sale was arranged to take place at 8.30am on 4 May, 1917, and duly advertised in the local media. Queues had begun to form a good three hours before the advertised opening time. The potatoes were on sale in units of 6lbs, enough therefore for up to 2,000 customers to have one unit each. But by the time the store opened more than twice that number had turned up, coming by foot, train and tram from

Part of the Great Potato Queue, estimated to number 5,000 people, of May, 1917

all over the county. Quickly appraising the situation, Leonard immediately arranged for another 2,000lbs to be transported. Even so, these and the original 12,000lbs had all been dispensed within the space of 90 minutes, thanks in part to the highly efficient distribution system supervised by the general manager himself.

The exercise was repeated two weeks later, this time involving 17,000lbs of potatoes bought from farms in Cambridgeshire, which Bentalls sold at the same price and just as quickly. If the episode won Leonard Bentall many new friends, it also attracted a degree of criticism – that it was against the interests of vegetable wholesalers and retailers, that it was none of Bentalls' business to be selling potatoes in the first place, and even that Bentalls were profiteering. Leonard was able to answer this last point emphatically, by displaying the receipt for the goods in his shop window. As to the other criticisms, the events leading up to his action provided ample justification; he no doubt would have argued that, had the Government enforced the fixed price more effectively, the situation would not have arisen. What is not in doubt is that, consciously or otherwise, it was a superb publicity *coup*.

The war over, Leonard was able to turn his attention once again to the business of expansion. George, his brother, had decided to retire and Herbert Perkins and Maurice Harcourt, who had been with Bentalls since 1902, were appointed joint managers. First to fall, as it were, was the previously immovable Clarence Arms immediately adjoining the store, giving it a continuous frontage in Clarence Street. It was the spur for a new Bentalls building which drew the following admiring headline from the *Surrey Comet*: GREATER LONDON'S GREATEST STORE, featuring as it did a spacious millinery department and an extensive department for new and second hand furniture, not to mention the latest in *gizmos*. They included a more sophisticated model of the Lamson tube, the improbably named Belt Desk Automatic Power Control Pneumatic Tube System. The new building also facilitated the expansion of a development introduced 10 years earlier, a tea room decorated in Moorish style, a very up-market innovation for the Kingston of 1907, with 'Sesame' doors which to the customers' amazement opened as they stood in front of them. This was now converted into a restaurant in the Olde English style and was the forerunner of a series of establishments in differing styles in the years that followed. One of them took its name from an old mulberry tree which stood in the walled garden of the vicarage in Wood Street. This, too, had been acquired by Bentalls immediately after the end of the War (not until the purchase had been authorised by the Archbishop of Canterbury), together with several other properties nearby.

There was an important change in the structure of the

'The Man Who Made Kingston'   Chapter 2

The corner of Wood Street and Clarence Street prior to the building of the new store in the late 1920s

business in 1925, two years after the death of its founder, Frank Bentall. It became a private limited company with a board comprising Leonard, Herbert Perkins, Maurice Harcourt, W Astles, who joined Bentalls in 1911 and had become merchandise manager, and Gerald Bentall, Leonard's elder son.

Hard on the heels of this development came the first real clash between the two leading forces in Kingston, Leonard Bentall and the Corporation, over the price of an item which the store used in large quantities to power many of its main attractions – electricity. There had been a row on the same subject a dozen years earlier in 1912, prompted by the fact that Kingston Corporation charged Bentalls a cheaper price for their supply than it charged a rival drapery and family firm, Wright Brothers. On the face of it the disparity seemed inequitable. However, Bentalls were by far the town's biggest consumer of electricity and Leonard had negotiated a deal whereby

Leonard Bentall's private office

Bentalls were charged 3.1 pence per unit until the middle of 1913 and 2.45 pence per unit for the following three years, together with a guaranteed payment of £2,300 over the period, whether Bentalls used this amount of electricity or not. But by 1925 Leonard decided the price the Council were then charging was too high. This time there was to be no compromise. Leonard was in the business of knowing that if customers were asked to pay what they considered too high a price for something, they would look elsewhere. He adopted a similar policy. In fact, he went further. He decided to make his own.

The engineer in him was no doubt absorbed in the undertaking, major by any standards and particularly for a company whose business was retailing. Completed within a year, it was an unqualified success, meeting all the store's needs and doing so for half the unit price Bentalls had been paying. It represented

'The Man Who Made Kingston' Chapter 2

a loss of income to the Corporation of more than £2,000 a year. More, it nurtured Leonard's fascination for innovations and the years that followed saw the introduction of calculating machines and machines for opening letters, operating windows, sun blinds and ventilators, washing dishes, polishing glasses and burnishing cutlery, all powered by electricity produced in the basement by the huge oil-fired engines.

Two years after they were first installed, early one winter's evening three weeks before Christmas, Bentalls shone like a lone beacon in the town. The Corporation's power supply had failed and Kingston was in darkness for several hours. Leonard must have permitted himself a smile, though he would have derived more satisfaction from the episode a decade later when a fault in a newly installed transformer at the town's power

Bentalls' electricity generating plant

31

station once again plunged Kingston into darkness. Within an hour, Bentalls had rigged up an emergency link to the local hospitals and kept them supplied until normal service was resumed.

Leonard next turned his attention to the motor car, an invention for which he had a life-long fascination. By this time, the fascination had begun to affect a significant proportion of the population as well and Leonard was quick to see that it was the means of bringing in new customers from a much wider catchment area. But how to attract them? Advertising and special promotions were already bringing Bentalls to the attention of a wider public than ever before. But something more was needed. His response was twofold; first, to provide them with a large new restaurant; secondly, and most imaginatively, to build a large covered car park for their vehicles.

The Tudor Restaurant was built on the site of the vicarage in Wood Street and, indeed, retained much of the original façade. It included spectacular murals recalling historic scenes from Kingston's past and some splendid stained glass windows depicting the emblems of England, Ireland, Scotland and Wales. The murals were plaster reliefs and the work of Hermon Cawthra, who exhibited at the Royal Academy for many years and who had executed the friezes of several London theatres, Sadlers Wells among them. The scenes in the Tudor restaurant at Bentalls showed: (i) the meeting between the Archbishop of Canterbury, local nobles and various bishops in 838 at the ecclesiastical court in Kingston at which was concluded the original Union of Church and State; (ii) the crowning of King Athelstan at Kingston in 924; (iii) King John granting Kingston's first charter in 1200; (iv) Henry VIII and Queen Anne Boleyn travelling up river from Kingston to Hampton Court in 1533; (v) insurrectionists under Sir Thomas Wyatt storming Kingston Bridge in 1554; (vi) Queen Elizabeth I

Five of the Hermon Cawthra murals for the Tudor Restaurant; a sixth is now at Kingston Grammar School

visiting Kingston with her courtiers in 1564 for the endowment of the grammar school; (vii) King Charles and his army at Kingston in 1642; and finally (viii) Jerry Abershaw, a noted 18th-century highwayman, holding up a coach on Wimbledon Common. When the Tudor restaurant was translated in the late 1960s into the Thames Room, the murals were taken down. Only one of them remains on view, the one showing Queen Elizabeth I which, appropriately enough, is at the foot of the staircase in the main entrance hall at Kingston Grammar School. There have been numerous links between the school and the store over the years (in the 1920s and 30s, Bentalls provided school meals there) and Edward Bentall, the present Chairman, is on the School's governing body. For the record, the remaining seven murals are stored away in the Bentalls furniture depository.

Despite a good deal of local scepticism, the restaurant was an immediate success. Within two years of opening in 1928 it was serving nearly 1,000 lunches and 1,500 teas on an average day, in addition to catering for private functions. So far was the idea ahead of its time that there was an even greater degree of scepticism over the car park, which was under construction on the opposite side of Wood Street close to where the present car park is located. It had necessitated the purchase of some cottages, an engineering works, several plots of land, and Down Hall, whose grounds extended to the river, some of which Leonard later donated to Kingston's thriving Sea Cadet unit and some he gave to the town to enable the road to be widened. Not only did it accommodate 450 customers' cars, it also housed the company's delivery vans which had been garaged next to the store, thus freeing space which could then be incorporated into the sales area. Like the restaurant, the car park was an immense success, with a daily turnover of over 1,000 vehicles on Saturdays and the necessity for its own in-house 'policeman' to direct traffic. It also incorporated a stand of petrol pumps and a workshop where customers could have their cars repaired whilst they shopped. Nor did Leonard miss the opportunity afforded by hundreds of square feet of empty wall space to turn them into advertising hoardings for Bentalls' merchandise. It was unique in the UK in that it was purpose-built as an undercover car park offering full repair and service facilities. Incidentally, its Wood Street elevation was designed by the Canadian architect Howard Crane.

Leonard's great plan to build a suburban store in which almost every essential to modern living could be had under the one roof was taking shape and the acquisition of land and properties continued, not just those adjoining the store but within the parameters of the present site. Among his latest acquisitions was the sub post office in Clarence Street which, far from closing, re-opened in the Bentalls store. It was one of the first examples of what is now a commonplace if sometimes controversial arrangement with Royal Mail for sub post offices to be run under licence. Moreover, it provided yet another new service for the benefit of Bentalls customers.

Inevitably, his land plan met with obstacles. One of the most formidable was a general store in Wood Street. Although the premises had been acquired by Bentalls, the sitting tenant had refused their offer of alternative premises close by. When the man's lease expired in 1930, Leonard, thwarted by this single obstruction, made a further offer – to re-house him 150 yards away at half his annual rent of £40 and to include new shop-fittings free of charge. Still the tenant refused, requesting £950 by way of compensation. The matter went to Kingston County Court, which found in Bentalls' favour, deciding there were no grounds for compensation and that, moreover, it was in the town's interest for the Bentalls development to proceed since it would provide jobs that were sorely needed.

The Grand Design could now unfold. What it entailed was the re-building of the store, no less. One of the most extraordinary aspects of the plan was its very timing, since Britain in 1930 was in the debilitating grip of the Depression. It was an act of Churchillian courage, characteristic of the man, to undertake such a massive expansion when all around him were drawing in their horns. By such men are recessions curtailed and business confidence renewed. Arguably, it was his greatest contribution to Kingston. Not only did it provide work for the construction industry and, on completion, for an extra 500 store staff. It also gave Kingston one of its most distinctive landmarks.

'Grand' was hardly an exaggeration, for the façade was modelled on the William and Mary wing of Hampton Court Palace designed by Sir Christopher Wren. It was an apt choice in as much as the palace is less than three miles upstream and over the centuries had provided Kingston's traders with a good deal of royal business. But it was an audacious scheme, calling for an exceptional talent to execute it. Leonard found the talent in one of the leading architects of the day, Maurice Webb of Sir Aston Webb and Sons. At first, even *he* was reportedly taken aback at what was in Leonard's mind, though not for long, and the 'Aston Webb façade' as it became known and which has been preserved to form an integral part of the present Bentall Centre is a tribute not only to Leonard's vision but also to Maurice Webb's skill. And what skill! It was one thing to design a 700ft long façade of brick and Portland stone five storeys high; it was another to build a new store on the sand and gravel that underlies Bentall's location so close to the banks of the Thames. The solution was to build the foundations on a raft of concrete strong enough to bear the weight of more than 2,000 tons of steelwork.

In addition to the Aston Webb façade, the building incorporated almost in its entirety the fine mock Tudor frontage of the former vicarage, as well as the Tudor restaurant built in 1928. The interior was as impressive as the exterior, albeit in a different way. The most striking feature of the Wood Street building of the 1930s, like the most striking feature of the Bentall Centre of the 1990s, was the vast hall (or atrium as we'd call it nowadays) with its glass roof and natural lighting, affording excellent views of large areas of the store. Pragmatists may argue that such voids are a waste of good selling space. Bentalls' experience suggests that customers prefer the feeling of openness and spaciousness and of being able to take in at a glance what is on offer without being pressured to buy by the confines of a small space. The present Kingston store, rebuilt in 1990, is modelled on these very lines. It also features the escalator connecting one floor to the next which in Leonard's day was a great novelty as he and Maurice Webb discovered in North America on a visit to department stores, forerunners of many such visits by teams from Bentalls which continue to this day. Incidentally, the stained glass which was one of the features of the escalator well and which was the work of a French artist, may now be seen over the Wood Street and bridge entrances to Bentalls' store.

As with the electricity generating plant and most of the machinery in the store, Leonard was determined that the escalators would be British made, despite the inconvenient fact that there was only one company manufacturing escalators in the whole of Europe and they were based in Berlin. For Leonard, this was simply a complication to be circumvented, which he duly did by contacting British engineering companies with appropriate expertise, among them the lift manufacturers Messrs J E Hall based in Dartford in Kent. With typical enterprise, Leonard flew to Germany and reached agreement for the escalators to be built by Halls under licence. In due course, the first escalators to be made in Britain were commissioned in the new store. Their use entailed a short learning course, first by Bentalls' staff – of whom there were now more than 1,000 – then by their customers, aided by a recorded message played on a gramophone at the foot of the unit which warned: '*Do not attempt to board the escalator without holding on to the rail! Dogs should be carried and umbrellas should be held clear!*'

Three years before the opening of the new store in 1935 the first phase of the re-building opened, its many notable features including two new departures, a food hall and ladies' hairdressing salon. In the meantime Leonard negotiated the most significant addition to the site so far, the purchase of White's mineral water factory in Fife Road representing a 20 per cent extension of the existing area occupied by Bentalls. It facilitated a reorganisation of several departments and also enabled a new entrance to be opened for the public. This Fife Road entrance was notable for its automatic doors operated by a photoelectric cell – a boon for ladies with prams for whom there was a double blessing in the shape of a pram park, complete with trained nurse, just inside. It was the first of its kind in a British store.

New techniques of a much more substantial nature were by now in use in the final construction phase of the new store. It was as crucial to Bentalls then as it was in the building of the new store in 1990 that trading continued uninterrupted by building work for as long as possible. This requirement presented the construction engineers with an acute problem, one that was compounded by the difficult terrain on which they were building. The foundations of the original store were laid on 15 feet of gravel and sand containing 12 feet of water with clay beneath; the foundations had to be replaced while the old building above continued in use. Adopting a system used in the building of the London Underground, chemicals were pumped in via large pipes. Like the modern day glues and hardeners, they solidified when mixed together to form a mass of exceptional strength which comfortably supported the store above. When it came to the foundations for the 1990s store, there was a new problem in that they were required to be six feet below water level, to which there was a new solution named 'shallow well pumping'. Used here for the first time in Britain, it entailed drilling bore holes to a depth of 30 feet below the level of the basement to enable the water to be pumped out.

The fitting out of the store provided yet another example of Leonard Bentall's resourcefulness. At about the time construction of the first phase in Kingston was under way, Gamages, owners of the well-known store in London's Holborn, opened a brand new store at the Marble Arch end of Oxford Street. Due to the depression and other factors it proved to be disaster and closed after six months. The fixtures and fittings, virtually brand new and of the latest design, were put up for auction. Leonard acquired every single item for the round sum of £65,000. They were duly transported to Kingston by what else but Bentalls' fleet of removal vans, and amounted to 341 van loads. The opportunity this cavalcade afforded to publicise Bentalls in London's West End was not lost on Leonard, who had special signage and posters produced for the purpose.

This was as nothing when compared with the fanfare of publicity which marked the opening of the new store on 9 September, 1935, performed every hour on the hour by trumpeters from the Coldstream Guards heralding two weeks of celebrations. One of the most successful features was a Radio-Bentalls exhibition based on the highly successful Radiolympia, featuring not only radios but also the latest television set and a machine which enabled customers to record themselves on an unbreakable disk for the price of 6d, as well as guest appearances by personalities from the world of entertainment. Top footballers and cricketers made personal appearances in the Sports Department. Some of the leading bands of the day played in the restaurant. On display was a working model of a Hoover vacuum cleaner 20 times larger than normal and a rose garden containing 5,000 blooms.

From start to finish it was a spectacular success and a splendid memorial to its instigator, and regarded as one of the greatest achievements in the history of store building. But Leonard Bentall was not quite finished. Two years before the opening of the new store, he had acquired a two acre site ¼ mile away in Cromwell Road with the object of building a furniture depository to serve the removals business and to replace the by now inadequate premises in Penrhyn Road. Nothing out of the ordinary in that, except that he commissioned Maurice Webb to design it. It was akin to asking Shakespeare to write a manual on car maintenance. The result is one of the most striking buildings in Kingston.

Its Italian Renaissance style, however incongruous and anachronistic it may seem, has provided Bentalls and indeed Kingston with a unique landmark and, since it is one of the tallest buildings in the town, one of the most visible. Indeed, it was widely condemned at the time as being out of scale with the surrounding landscape (a criticism it shared with St Paul's Cathedral) and many thought that Leonard had overstepped the bounds of architectural decency. Nevertheless its lines were commemorated in a drawing which was hung in the Royal Academy in 1936 and its interior was a minor masterpiece of design and engineering. Lifts took the incoming removal vans to one of the six floors on which furniture was stored. Thick steel doors provided protection against fire. Special guttering and hollow walls provided protection against damp. The roof was insulated with cork to provide protection against excessive variations in temperature. All in all it was a masterpiece, practically as well as architecturally.

Devoted as Leonard's life was to Bentalls, still he had time to enjoy a full family life as well as some leisure time pursuits, gardening and golf among them. But he also had an acute sense of the needs of others who were less fortunate. His concern for the welfare of his own staff is documented in a later chapter. He expended his prodigious energies, too, outside the immediate Bentalls family. The first beneficiary was the trade itself, through the medium of the Warehousemen, Clerks' and Drapers' Schools which had been founded in 1853 for the children of 'deceased and necessitous employees' and which was based at Purley in Surrey. In the early 1920s it was decided to build additional premises at nearby Addington to accommodate 80 boys of 11 years of age and over, leaving 170 girls and 60 younger boys at Purley. In many cases, the children had lost parents in the First World War.

Having served two years as chairman of the appeal committee for the Greater London area, in 1922 Leonard – by then busily engaged with the new store – was elected the youngest president of the national appeal committee. Typically, he brought a fresh approach to the business of fund raising. In identifying previous sources of donations he discovered most came from the London stores and the wholesalers and comparatively little from the provinces, even though 50 per cent of the youngsters in the Schools came from outside London. He discovered, too, that most of the approaches for donations in the past had been by letter. So he planned a fund raising campaign based on personal visits to every town of more than 10,000 inhabitants in England, Scotland and Wales. In the space of a year or so he travelled more than 6,000 miles by car, driven by his faithful chauffeur, Tapper. By April 1923, the staggering and record-breaking sum of just over £52,000 (equivalent to £1.4 million at today's values) had been raised during his year and in recognition of his remarkable achievement Leonard was presented with an illuminated commemorative album, still treasured by the Bentall family.

The Addington school was opened by the Prince of Wales the following year. It was designed by Sir Aston Webb, thus beginning an association which culminated in the opening of the new Bentall store in 1935 and the furniture depository a year earlier. Leonard went on to chair the Schools' aftercare committee whose task was to try to ensure that the youngsters found jobs in the trade. The Bentall family involvement continued until 1973 when the Addington school was sold to the Royal Russell School Society for more than £1-million.

Leonard was also involved in fund raising for a holiday and convalescent home for shop assistants at Bexhill-on-Sea, the Roberts Marine Mansion, and in the building of a new mansion at Worthing opened by Princess Alice. On the day of the opening, as Leonard, driven as ever by Tapper, approached the new building, he saw that the flag on the flagpole in the grounds had dropped to half mast. Tapper was promptly commissioned to scamper up the pole and put things to rights. He earned Leonard's thanks – and a mild rebuke for soiling his new livery . . .

The next beneficiary of Leonard's charitable activities was the sea cadet corps in Kingston, of whose founding committee he was a member. The corps took its name from the *Steadfast*, a brig which it bought as a training ship in 1911. Leonard became chairman of the Steadfast Sea Cadet Corps in 1921, from which date the unit advanced in leaps and bounds, winning a wardroom full of trophies including, most notably, Lord Jellicoe's Battle for Jutland sword in 1929 in competition with members of the Navy League throughout the British Empire. In subsequent years Leonard's sons succeeded one another as president of the corps which, in 1957 and again in 1973, won the Canada Trophy awarded to the top unit in the country. Leonard's grandson Edward is the Corps' current chairman.

As Leonard's reputation as a fund raiser spread, so others sought out his support. In 1927, for example, the YMCA (Young Men's Christian Association) in Kingston found itself short of funds to the tune of £4,000 for its new £6,000 headquarters building and approached Leonard, who had been associated with the movement for a number of years, to become its president and chairman of its finance committee. His response was swift and characteristic; if the committee could raise £1,750 by the end of the year (just four weeks away) he would pledge £750. The money was raised – and the balance, not long afterwards – and Leonard was presented with an illuminated scroll of acknowledgement by Princess Helena Victoria. Leonard continued to serve the organisation for another five years as chairman of the management committee.

He was active in other fields, too, being one of the instigators of the Richmond Park golf course, the first public course to be opened in the vicinity of London. It was a condition of the development, however, that it should be built entirely by private subscription and Leonard was one of the management committee who pledged £6,000 to enable it to proceed. The course was designed by J H Taylor – with James Braid and Harry Vardon, one of the Great Triumvirate of British golf at the beginning of this century – and opened by the Prince of Wales in 1923. Some 100,000 rounds of golf were played on the 18 hole course in the first year, prompting Leonard to suggest to the management committee the need for a second course. His proposal was adopted and the new course was opened, two years later, by the then Duke of York, later to become King George VI, the two courses becoming knows as the Prince's and the Duke's. At about the same time Leonard, who was vice-president of a nine hole course at Maundesley-on-Sea,

Opening of Richmond Park Golf Course by HRH the Prince of Wales

initiated its extension into an 18-hole course which Harry Vardon supervised.

Golf nearly landed Bentalls in court. The cause was an aeroplane towing a streamer proclaiming 'Bentalls for Fine Furnishing', a familiar enough form of advertising in the 1930s, which flew over a golf course where a match on which a sizeable wager had been staked was taking place. As one of the participants was lining up a crucial putt, the shadow of the streamer passed across the green. The putt missed the hole and the match was lost. The loser then attempted to sue Bentalls, threatening to spawn a whole industry in sports litigation. (How the matter was resolved is unrecorded; perhaps the plaintiff reconciled himself to the unpalatable truth facing all golfers, that when we miss a putt, the fault is nobody's but our own.)

Leonard was by all accounts an enthusiastic, if only average, golfer. He also had an enthusiasm for gardening and for overseas travel. Many of his foreign holidays were punctuated by a series of acquisitions made for Bentalls en route. In Egypt he met Howard Carter, discoverer of Tutankhamun's tomb, and acquired a life-size replica of the boy king's throne. Inevitably, it formed part of a 'special promotion' at Bentalls and was sold at a later date at Christies for £1,000. In North America he negotiated the first consignment of the Canada First brand of canned fruit and vegetables in the UK. From his 'grand tour' around the world in 1936 he sent back from Honolulu 100 cases of pineapples and, from New Zealand, innumerable tins of Rotorowa soup – all with the instructions that they had to be sold before his return to the store. In most cases his staff were able to comply. The Rotorowa soup was an exception to this rule. Made from an oyster flavoured fish with a very pronounced taste it was not the hit in Kingston that undoubtedly it is in its native land. By the time Leonard returned, most of the tins remained unsold, so he assumed personal responsibility for its marketing. It must go down as one of his few failures – finally making its exit via the directors' dining room where it featured on the menu several times a week, to the dismay of his colleagues on the board.

Fish soup apart, his return to Kingston at the end of the four month world trip in 1937 was a glittering occasion, marked by a ball held in the store in honour of Leonard and his wife and attended by 1,200 Bentalls employees. To a fanfare by trumpeters of the Coldstream Guards, they entered beneath a flower-decked canopy held by six girls. A band played *Home Sweet Home*, neon lights flashed 'Welcome Home' and a huge, illuminated map picked out the places they had visited during their trip. Leonard must have been tickled pink. His acknowledgement, in which incidentally he refers to some of the nicknames by which he was known, ended thus:

THE MEN WHO MADE KINGSTON

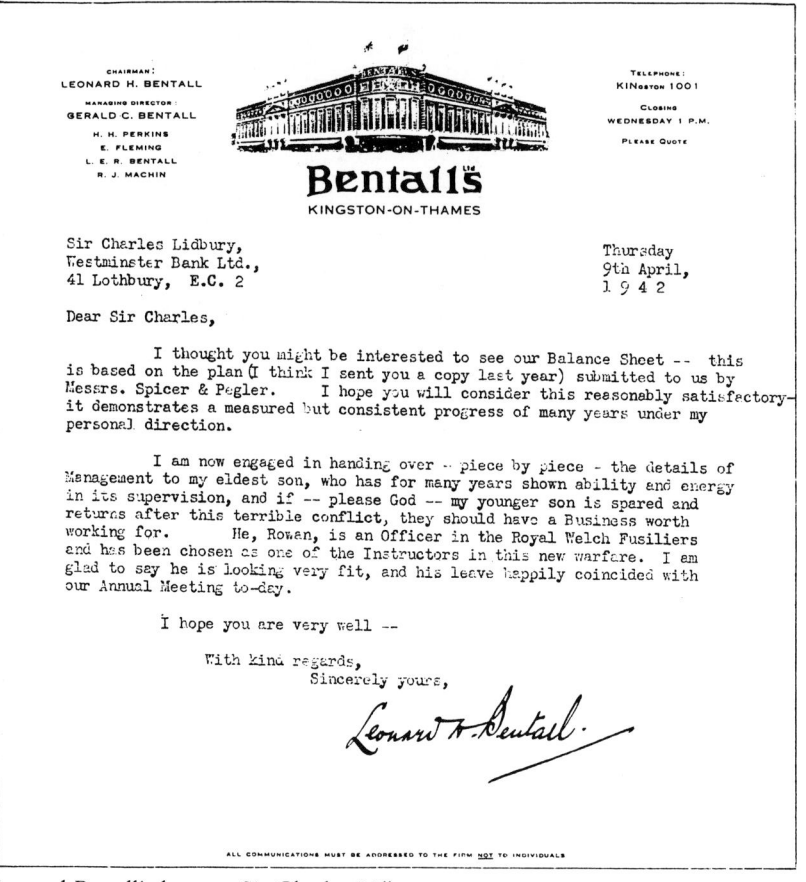

> **CHAIRMAN:**
> LEONARD H. BENTALL
> **MANAGING DIRECTOR:**
> GERALD C. BENTALL
> H. H. PERKINS
> E. FLEMING
> L. E. R. BENTALL
> R. J. MACHIN
>
> **Bentalls** LTD
> KINGSTON-ON-THAMES
>
> **TELEPHONE:**
> KINGSTON 1001
> **CLOSING**
> WEDNESDAY 1 P.M.
> PLEASE QUOTE
>
> Sir Charles Lidbury,
> Westminster Bank Ltd.,
> 41 Lothbury, E.C. 2
>
> Thursday
> 9th April,
> 1942
>
> Dear Sir Charles,
>
>   I thought you might be interested to see our Balance Sheet -- this is based on the plan (I think I sent you a copy last year) submitted to us by Messrs. Spicer & Pegler. I hope you will consider this reasonably satisfactory-- it demonstrates a measured but consistent progress of many years under my personal direction.
>
>   I am now engaged in handing over - piece by piece - the details of Management to my eldest son, who has for many years shown ability and energy in its supervision, and if -- please God -- my younger son is spared and returns after this terrible conflict, they should have a Business worth working for. He, Rowan, is an Officer in the Royal Welch Fusiliers and has been chosen as one of the Instructors in this new warfare. I am glad to say he is looking very fit, and his leave happily coincided with our Annual Meeting to-day.
>
> I hope you are very well --
>
>   With kind regards,
>   Sincerely yours,
>
>   Leonard H. Bentall.
>
> ALL COMMUNICATIONS MUST BE ADDRESSED TO THE FIRM NOT TO INDIVIDUALS

Leonard Bentall's letter to Sir Charles Lidbury

'You have all heard a considerable amount about 'A merchant venturer' and perhaps a little about 'the phantom king of Kingston' but in my heart I would rather you knew me as a friend, and a deep friend, of you all. The more I travelled the more I felt the necessity of keeping close to one another. I cannot do without any one of you, and I do not want any one of you to do without me, and if in the few years that remain to me as head of this business I can be of any added service to any one, or as many as like to take the advantage, I am determined to do so in every way which lies in my power.'

Leonard Bentall died on Christmas Eve, 1942, at the age of 67. Nine months earlier he had written to Sir Charles Lidbury, Chief General Manager of Westminster Bank, the Company's bankers, enclosing a copy of the latest balance sheet, adding:

'I am now engaged in handing over – piece by piece – the details of Management to my eldest son, who has for many years shown ability and energy in its supervision, and if – please God – my younger son is spared and returns after this terrible conflict, they should have a Business worth working for. He, Rowan, is an Officer in the Royal Welsh Fusiliers and has been chosen as one of the Instructors in this new warfare. I am glad to say he is looking very fit, and his leave happily coincided with our Annual Meeting to-day.'

A day or two later Sir Charles replied: 'Thank you for sending me a copy of the Company's accounts for the year ended 31st January 1942, and I do congratulate you on the excellent results shown which reflect so much your able guidance and direction of the business.

'You must, I know, feel very proud of your stewardship and I do most sincerely express the hope that nothing will arise to prevent your sons succeeding to that stewardship in the fullness of time. Certainly they have had a wonderful example of initiative, drive and enterprise in their father and I hope they will be the happy inheritors of his great qualities.

'I am pleased to say I am keeping well and I hope you are too, notwithstanding the difficulties and anxieties which must be yours during these troublesome times.'

The memory of Leonard Hugh Bentall is preserved in a hundred and one different manifestations of his vision and enterprise, in several portraits, and in the larger-than-life size statue which gazes across the great open atrium of the Bentall Centre. It epitomises his favourite phrase: 'The way lies ever ahead'. The bronze statue was commissioned from the sculptor Sir

THE MEN WHO MADE KINGSTON

Portrait of Leonard Bentall (undated) by W S Stuart

William Reid Dick. At the foot was the inscription: 'Leonard Hugh Bentall, 1875 – 1942, to whose organising genius and dynamic personality this store owes its great success'. Many tributes were paid to Leonard at the unveiling ceremony, including these words by the Lord Lieutenant of Surrey, Sir Malcolm Fraser: 'As Napoleon learned to his cost, this country, which he called 'a nation of shopkeepers', was a country of shopkeepers possessed of matchless initiative and the courage of their convictions. Leonard Hugh Bentall was just such a one as these. He was a local pioneer whose many charitable actions will long be remembered. In addition he was a man of high adventure, with ability to mould the materials at his hand into a great and prosperous business.'

But the most apt tribute of all was from the Mayor of Kingston, Cllr F C Digby. He described Leonard Bentall as 'The man who made Kingston'.

3. Bentalls Upon Thames

THE BENTALLS EFFECT ON THE TOWN OF KINGSTON

Over the decades, the contribution made by Bentalls to the town of Kingston has been immense. The store has acted like a magnet, attracting customers from far and wide into the town. Bentalls have provided jobs for many living in the vicinity; at one period, they employed as many as 3,500 people, making them one of the largest employers in Kingston. Their on-going series of expansion programmes have provided work for those in the building and other trades, most significantly during the depression years of the 1930s when the predecessor of the present store was being built. As one of the biggest single ratepayers, they have contributed large sums into the town's coffers. They have provided business for many local service organisations – banks, insurance companies, and many others. Local shops have found themselves with new customers, drawn to the town by the presence of the store. And Bentalls' buildings, in particular the Aston Webb façade of the store, the Italian Renaissance styling of the furniture depository and the spacious interior of the Bentall Centre, have added dignity, elegance and variety to the Kingston scene.

Without Bentalls, it might be argued, Clarence Street, Wood Street and Fife Road would still be a collection of shops, pubs, a brewery, a school and a vicarage, leaving the town without the focal point which has made its reputation as a shopping centre since the early part of this century.

Through the variety and range of their merchandise, Bentalls have added to the quality of life of countless people in the town and done so at prices most can afford. The competitiveness of their pricing has been a key part of their philosophy since the days of Frank Bentall and remains so today. Rowan Bentall mentions those early days in *My Store of Memories* writing about a Mrs Susanna Fowler who was born at about the time Frank Bentall established his shop. 'As a teenage girl she used to earn five shillings a week in a Kingston guest house – and with this she was expected to supplement the family's income. She often visited Bentalls to look around but only seldom could she buy; in fact the most she ever bought was a yard or two of material at 4d a yard with which to make a dress. She married in the early 1890s, when my father first went into the business, but she remained a loyal customer of Bentalls, always receiving courteous service. She eventually had nine children to bring up while her husband's earnings never exceeded £3 5s a week during the whole of her married life. To maintain even a modest standard in food and clothing Mrs Fowler had to take in other people's washing and she also made trousers at 6d a pair. But she still managed to scrape together a few coppers every few weeks to buy material from Bentalls plus the occasional hat and stockings – black for everyday wear and white, with patterns up the side, for special occasions.' There were hundreds of customers like Mrs Fowler for whom Bentalls catered, in addition to those at the top end of the market. Indeed, for many years after the business had become a department store, the basement with its bargains and its pots and pans was a realm into which the more affluent customers rarely ventured.

As well as caring for their customers, Bentalls have added hugely to their entertainment and that of the population at large through the variety of their special promotions. An obvious example was the series of Christmas circus processions of the early 1950s. Not all their initiatives were directly related to promoting the sale of merchandise. One of the most recent was the D-Day Remembered exhibition in 1994. Since a great many members of Bentalls' staff had served in the Second World War, and since large numbers of the allied forces had been billeted nearby in Bushey Park before heading for the coast, the company were keen to commemorate the D-Day landings. Bentalls had arranged with the British Army Museum at Chelsea Barracks jointly to produce some panels for use at the exhibition and afterwards at the Museum. Quite by chance, during the planning stages one of Bentalls' managers, Derek Honour, received an appeal from Bushey Park for help in funding new plantings for the commemorative Eisenhower Copse. Bentalls were delighted to help and, in return, were put in touch with the Museum of Richmond which was invaluable in supplying Bentalls with information and artefacts for their exhibition. The items included gas masks, Home Guard uniforms and helmets, ration books and a bomb found on Ham Common. The opening of the exhibition was attended by about 30 local war veterans who were impressed by the detailed information, photographs and maps on display. HRH Princess Alexandra visited the exhibition. To entice younger visitors to the exhibition, a WWII Jeep, lent by the British Army Museum, was on display at the ground floor entrance, and a US Army band performed in the Bentalls Centre. Bentalls' sponsorship was graciously acknowledged in the foreword to *Monty's Men: The British Soldier and the D-Day Campaign* by Julian Humphrys, published the same year.

As part of the celebrations to mark the centenary of the store in 1967, Bentalls staged a veteran car rally, the route being from Kingston to Worthing and back, ending with lunch in the store's Tudor Restaurant. On the last leg of the journey there was a dramatic thunderstorm accompanied by torrential rain. Most of the competitors, who were members of the South East Veteran Car Club, got rather damp and were provided with dry socks and slippers straight from the store. After the rally, several of the veteran cars were put on display in the store's windows.

Thanks to Bentalls, the people of Kingston and further afield have had an opportunity of meeting all kinds of celebrities who have performed in the store, opened exhibitions or signed books there. The pattern was established back in the 1930s, one of the first celebrities being the Lancashire Cotton Queen of 1933 who added a royal seal of approval to a successful sewing exhibition in the store. One of the best remembered from these early years was the Swedish high diver Anita Kittner who astonished the crowds in the famous Escalator Hall with her plunges into a tiny pool from a height of 60 feet.

The sports department was a constant draw, starting in the 1930s with appearances by leading personalities from the fields of table tennis, soccer, billiards and cricket. The two celebrated Maurices, Tate and Leyland, gave coaching sessions there in 1936. Ten years later there was a series of Cricket Fortnights when the Bedser twins, Alec and Eric, who were friends of Rowan Bentall, brought along fellow professionals from the Surrey club to bowl at any aspiring batsmen among the customers. The demand was so great that a restriction had to be placed on the number of balls each could receive. Then there were the famous mannequin parades, so popular indeed that a special room, known as the Mannequin Hall, was built to accommodate them. The hall, later known as the Wolsey Hall

Bentalls Upon Thames   *Chapter 3*

Alec Bedser (seated) and his twin Eric at one of the many book signings

and Cromwell Suite, was also used for banquets, weddings, receptions, dinners and dances. But of its prime role, Rowan Bentall in *My Store of Memories* writes thus: 'Shortly after it was opened a series of lavish mannequin parades were held twice daily at 3pm and 5pm. These were a great attraction since, in addition to Bentalls' own mannequins, several stars of the London mannequin circuit were drafted in, including Lucie Clayton, whose hair was insured for £1,000, Betty Spurling, whose smile was insured for £1,000, Joanne Safelle, London's tallest mannequin – whose height was not, as far as I know, insured for anything – Vera Fleck, winner of the Gainsborough Film Star competition and Betty Soldan, best known as the original Palmolive girl'.

Since then there have been personalities from all walks of life visiting the store to sign copies of their books or records. The list reads like a Who's Who of showbiz personalities and in recent years has included (with apologies to those whose names inadvertently may have been omitted):

Muhammad Ali	Robert Dougall	Dame Vera Lynn
Eamonn Andrews	Noel Edmonds	Sir Robert Mark
Jeffrey Archer	Gareth Edwards	Alan Minter
Arthur Askey	Keith Floyd	Frank Muir
Sir David Attenborough	Margot Fonteyn	John Nettles
	Julia Foster	Anne Nightingale
Pam Ayres	Dick Francis	Derek Nimmo
Richard Baker	John Francome	John Noakes
Tom Baker	Lady Antonia Frazer	Richard O'Sullivan
Michael Barry	Clement Freud	Gary Player
Bill Beaumont	Stephen Fry	Mary Quant
Duke & Duchess of Bedford	Bamber Gascoigne	Esther Rantzen
	The Goodies	Robin Ray
Alec & Eric Bedser	David Gower	Ted Ray
David Bellamy	Russell Grant	Mike Reid
Colonel John Blashford-Snell	Dulcie Gray	Sir Cliff Richard
	Larry Grayson	Sir Alec Rose
Reginald Bosanquet	Tony Hart	Willie Rushton
Geoffrey Boycott	Sir Edward Heath	Vidal Sasson
Richard Briers	Frankie Howerd	Donald Sinden
Trevor Brooking	Rod Hull	Delia Smith
Max Bygraves	Sir Len Hutton	Ed Stewart
Donald Campbell	Tony Jacklin	Una Stubbs
Willie Carson	Lena Kennedy	Leslie Thomas
Petula Clark	Robin Knox-Johnson	Alan Titchmarsh
Joan Collins	Danny La Rue	Alan Whicker
Henry Cooper	Robert Lacey	Kenneth Williams
Ronnie Corbett	Sue Lawley	Ernie Wise
Colin Cowdrey	Bernard Levin	Terry Wogan
John Curry	Martyn Lewis	Steve Wright
Michael Dennison	Maureen Lipman	Michael York
Placido Domingo	Lulu	Susannah York

All made their mark in various ways. Cliff Richard attracted hundreds of adoring fans. The record for the number of books sold during a signing – 750 copies – is still held by Sir David Attenborough. Waiting time for Placido Domingo's signature averaged over an hour and nearly £2,000 worth of his records were bought; he spent two and a quarter hours patiently signing them all. Sir Edward Heath visited twice and, as retired Bentalls director David Fowler recalls: 'He contributed enormously to our well-being as we were instructed to have Glenfiddich malt whisky on tap – which we did for months *after* his visit'. In the event, the former Tory Prime Minister sipped dry sherry. But none was more popular than actress Joan Collins whose first 'official' visit to the store came in the early 1980s, before she achieved international stardom, when she switched on Bentalls' Christmas lights. Her return in 1994 to sign copies of her book *My Secrets* eclipsed by some margin all previous book signings; shoppers packed in their hundreds into every available niche in the store and over 250 copies of the book were sold in the space of an hour.

Countless local charities have benefited from the patronage of the store and of members of the Bentalls family. Leonard was one of the founders and great benefactors of the Kingston Steadfast Sea Cadet Corps, to the local YMCA and to numerous charities further afield. His generosity to local organisations was emulated by his son, Rowan, who also served as President of Steadfast. Rowan helped in raising over £300,000 for the Elizabeth Fitzroy Homes for the Mentally Handicapped at Richmond and he was a trustee of the New Victoria Hospital, Kingston. In 1971 he convinced the Vicar of Kingston Parish Church that an appeal should be started to raise funds for the church tower, pledging his own and Bentalls' support. As a trustee of the General Charitable Trust at Kingston Grammar School he attended meetings regularly and when a trustee of

Joan Collins at the book signing in 1994

Kingston Arts Trust he worked closely with the Council and other bodies to organise a reception and exhibition of local arts. As Vice-President and then President, he gave active support and help to Kingston Rugby Football Club. Perhaps his greatest charitable achievement was to head the Kingston Hospital Scanner Appeal. In an appreciation of Rowan Bentall soon after his death in 1993, given at a celebration service at Kingston Parish Church, Peter Jarvis, Chairman of the Scanner Appeal, said that having decided Rowan would be the ideal person to be Appeal President he sounded out Rowan's son Edward. The latter, 'trying to let me down lightly,' said he thought it extremely unlikely his father would accept since he was then 80 and was looking forward to spending more time in the country with his family. Rowan, on the contrary, responded with enthusiasm and immediately got down to planning the launch. As Peter Jarvis remarked: 'His constant, generous and determined encouragement was just what my small group of volunteers needed to carry them through what appeared at first to be an impossible task. At the time of his death the miracle had almost been achieved.' Just a few weeks after the service, in fact, the target of £1-million was reached and, in recognition of his presidency and appreciation of his support, the building housing the scanner was named the Rowan Bentall Wing. It was opened by Her Royal Highness Princess Alexandra on 3 March, 1994.

Bentalls helped sponsor the Kingston Regatta in 1991, giving the event a higher profile than in any of its previous 135 years. Four years earlier they had become the first company to sponsor a series of summer evening entertainments for the National Trust at Claremont Landscape Gardens at Esher. The theme was the 'toe tapping twenties' and it attracted enthusiastic crowds, most of whom dressed for the part and arrived with picnic hampers, candelabra and flowers and dined *al fresco* around the lake.

THE MEN WHO MADE KINGSTON

Under the auspices of the Professional Golfers' Association, Bentalls organised a charity golf pro-am at Royal Mid-Surrey Golf Club in 1990 in aid of the Dysart School, a special school for children with severe learning difficulties serving the Kingston area. The event raised £10,000 and helped to provide a new roof and modern heating plant for the school's swimming pool, thus enabling it to be used for therapy for the multiple-handicapped children all year round.

Bentalls raised the architectural tone of the town through the elegance of the Hampton Court styling of their 1930s built store and the Italianate elegance of the furniture depository. In other ways, too, they have been patrons of the arts to the benefit of the community. An example was the commissioning of a huge mural for the escalator hall of the Kingston store by ex RAF fighter pilot Stefan Knapp in 1954. The artist was a Pole who had made an audacious escape from prison camp in Siberia and had served in the RAF as a fighter pilot, later studying at the Slade School of Art. The purpose of the mural was to decorate the large wall built of brick at the back of the escalator well. The commissioning led to the publication of a monograph, *Image of Kingston*, written by James Laver, worth reproducing for its brief commentary on the history of arts patronage.

> *Most people, nowadays, when they think of a painting think of a fairly small rectangle of canvas inside a frame. It may be in an exhibition with a host of other paintings, or on the wall of one's own home. One may like it very much, and even have made a considerable sacrifice to buy it; but one didn't ask the artist to paint it. And, of course, it bears no relation to its immediate surroundings or to the architecture of one's house.*
>
> *This kind of painting – easel painting as it is called – is a comparatively new thing. In earlier ages painting was not like that. It was an essential part of the building that contained it – temple*

Bentalls Upon Thames   *Chapter 3*

or palace. In a word, it was mural painting: the decoration of a wall. The ancient Egyptians filled every inch of their temple walls with figures. So did the builders of the great cathedrals of the Middle Ages; although most of them are now so scraped and bare that it is difficult to believe it. And the merchant-princes of Venice called in the greatest artists of their day to decorate their palaces, just as the Pope employed Michelangelo to cover the ceiling of the Sistine Chapel.

Many a modern painter must have sighed for such an opportunity, have grown discontented with the limitations of the easel-picture, and longed for a chance to work on a larger scale. But such opportunities are, in a modern world, extremely rare. It is true that there has been a revival of mural painting within recent years, especially in America; and even in England, some new churches have been built, and artists commissioned to cover their walls with images.

It is all a question of what used to be called patronage. No artist can produce a mural painting on his own responsibility and in his own studio. Somebody must offer him a wall and take the risk that what he paints on it will be to the patron's liking. Our churches are, in general, too poor, our merchant-princes too uncertain of the future to do this. Patronage has passed to other hands and so it must be a source of satisfaction to everyone who is interested in the Arts when the challenge is taken up by one of our great Stores.

Mr Stefan Knapp was commissioned to decorate Bentalls' main hall of their store with a mural painting. Mr Knapp is a young artist who was a fighter pilot during the war and who afterwards studied at the Slade School; he had already made a name for himself as a painter when this big opportunity came his way. And a big opportunity it is in every sense of the word, for the canvas affixed to the wall measures approximately 40ft by 40ft, and is probably the largest in England.

The non-naturalistic treatment may puzzle those who are accus-

tomed to more conventional handling. What the artist has tried to do is to evoke an image of Kingston and its surroundings with Bentalls store in the heart of the town by means of a series of symbols; the Thames coursing past fishermen who in their nets hold the three fishes of Kingston's coat-of-arms; three boatmen, one holding an oar; two bridges leading into Kingston, an invading horseman, the neighbouring Hampton Court Palace, a shepherd with his flock; and these symbols he has built up into a flat pattern which relies for its effect upon the interlocking shapes of brilliant colour. It is interesting to note the way in which the shapes reflect as it were the structure of the store and how the colours harmonise with the tinted glass in the roof. A work of this magnitude deserves something more than a passing glance which many will bestow upon it. It is a serious attempt to offer a new field to the artist and to relate the age-old art of mural painting to the conditions of the modern world.

Some years later the wall was knocked down to make way for the eastwards extension of the store to Fife Road, the huge canvas mural rolled up and put into storage where it remains.

In a different context it was Bentalls, in conjunction with their development partners in the Bentall Centre, Norwich Union, and the main contractors, John Mowlem, who bore the cost of moving the Coronation Stone from near the Guildhall to the Wood Street corner of All Saint's churchyard, immediately opposite the Bentall Centre. The stone, on which seven Anglo Saxon kings are believed to have been crowned, was moved in 1992 to coincide with a visit to Kingston by Her Majesty the Queen. During her visit she was escorted by Rowan Bentall round an exhibition explaining the role of the Bentall Centre in the regeneration of Kingston's town centre.

Then there was the contribution made by Bentalls to Hawker Siddeley, the Kingston based aircraft manufacturers, which

Bentalls Upon Thames   *Chapter 3*

entailed staging an exhibition in 1976 which facilitated the first Hawk aircraft order abroad, worth £128-million. Sir Colin Chandler, now Chief Executive of Vickers PLC, who was Commercial Director of Hawker Siddeley at the time, remembers the circumstances well. 'We were in fierce competition for a jet trainer for the Finnish Air Force with five other nations, including France, Sweden and the USA. The Hawk was new, having just entered service with the RAF, and this first overseas order was crucial. The Finns were looking for a reciprocal deal that would benefit their economy and I hit on the idea of

Part of the Friendly Finland display

approaching Bentalls to see whether they would be prepared to promote Finnish products through their store. The two companies had a long-standing relationship ever since the War when Bentalls helped Hawkers out by storing large assemblies for Hurricanes for which there was not enough space in the factory. I met Rowan Bentall and members of the board and I was very struck by their enthusiasm and determination to help us, as well as by their sincerity. They put together a team of buyers and we flew out to Finland. The result was the Friendly Finland Fortnight which sold a considerable quantity of furniture and other merchandise through the store. It may not have been quite to the value of the aircraft order, but it was a marvellous public relations exercise the benefits of which far outweighed the financial value. It set the seal on the order which saw the Hawk on its way to being one of the most successful British aircraft ever made.' Sir Colin later presented Bentalls with a silver replica of the Hawk, to accompany one of a Hurricane given them in appreciation for their wartime contribution.

Friendly Finland was just one of a host of immensely successful special promotions which have been a Bentalls hallmark over the years. They included two rather special events, Italy in Kingston in 1955 and Italia Romantica 15 years later, as the result of which the insignia of the Order Al Merito della Republica Italiana was awarded to Rowan Bentall by the President of Italy.

In other ways, too, Bentalls have had a profound effect on the Town and its development. The influence could have been even greater had the city fathers heeded their advice, especially in the matter of the bridge.

Kingston has had a bridge since Roman times, when it was the first crossing point of the Thames up river from London, hence the town's importance. After the Romans came the Saxons. Typical of a race who scorned such Roman necessities as hot baths and central heating, they destroyed the bridge and built a new one. Years later the bridge fell into such disrepair that traffic regularly resorted to crossing the river by boat when it was closed. Tolls were levied to help patch it up, but by the early 1800s the wooden structure was getting beyond repair and a new bridge was proposed. But who was going to bear the huge cost? Kingston Corporation's solution was to demand that the counties of Surrey and Middlesex foot the bill. The matter went to court, the Corporation lost the case and a good deal of money in legal costs. Substantial funding was then needed, not merely to meet the cost of constructing the bridge but for the purchase of properties to facilitate proper approaches to it, since it had been decided to site it 50 yards upstream of the original bridge. In 1825 the Corporation secured an Act of Parliament enabling it to raise the required funding by the imposition of tolls. Even so there was a need to make economies, and no less a personage than Thomas Telford, the celebrated engineer, was called in to confirm that the use of brick instead of stone for the internal piers would provide a sufficiently permanent structure, thereby reducing its total construction cost of £28,000 by some £4,500. In 1828, some 40 years before Frank Bentall's arrival in Kingston, the new bridge which was to help make Clarence Street* the most important in the town was opened by the Duchess of Clarence. The cost of the bridge having been recouped (and doubtless more besides), the bridge was freed from toll in 1870.

Usage of the bridge increased steadily over the years to keep pace with population increases on both sides of the river and the introduction of trams, so much so that the need to increase its capacity became imperative. In 1914, a major scheme to

* Initially it was called New Bridge Street but later re-named in honour of the Duchess.

widen the bridge, virtually doubling its width from nearly 30 feet to some 55 feet, was proposed and implemented. In effect, it added a second bridge to the first, providing for two lanes of traffic into Kingston and two out.

By the first part of the present decade, like other Thames bridges of its generation, it was beginning to show its age. Bricks had been displaced or cracked, chiefly as the result of water penetration and frost damage. By 1994 it was in urgent need of repair.

Bentalls had foreseen problems with the bridge years earlier when Kingston Council was considering proposals for a relief road which Bentalls' directors considered inadequate. So they decided to commission, at the company's expense, an eminent traffic consultant called Minoprio to produce an alternative plan.

The Minoprio plan proposed another crossing of the river via a second Kingston bridge, within sight of the existing bridge, to take through traffic. It was a bold and no doubt expensive solution. Unfortunately, it failed to commend itself to the Council, or, inexplicably, the local Chamber of Trade, and even less to the residents of Hampton Wick on the opposite bank of the river who were appalled at the prospect of one end of the bridge finishing up in their back yard, to say nothing of the problem of approach roads to it. There was bitter fighting within Kingston Council and between the Council and Bentalls, who saw it as the salvation to the town's ever pressing traffic problems and who were even prepared to give the Council some of their land with no strings attached to facilitate the scheme, an altruistic gesture which was never taken up. Thus Bentalls lost the battle. But when the problem of the bridge came home to roost in the 1990s they had some justification in feeling it could have been ameliorated had their proposal for a second crossing been adopted.

In 1994 a feasibility study was carried out to consider options for refurbishing the structure. The guiding principles were that, since the bridge has a Grade II star listing, the external appearance should remain generally unchanged and that remedial works should avoid causing excessive disruption to traffic and the local business and residential community. Five main options were advanced in the feasibility report. The first was for the minimum necessary refurbishment combined with the imposition of a permanent 3-tonnes weight limit. This entailed a construction cost of some £170,000 but also anticipated substantial user delay costs. The second was for a limited amount of strengthening combined with a permanent weight limit of 17-tonnes, thus enabling buses to use the bridge. Construction costs in this case were estimated at approximately £1.5-million, with fairly substantial user delay costs. Option C was for the full strengthening of the bridge at a cost of about £1.8-million with traffic usage reduced to two lanes during the refurbishment period.

The two last options were more adventurous in that they entailed the building of a temporary bridge parallel to the existing bridge to enable traffic to continue to flow during refurbishment, the first option proposing a four lane temporary bridge and the second a two lane temporary structure. Inevitably, construction costs in both cases were very much higher than for any of the other options (£3.9-million in the case of the four lane temporary bridge and £3.4-million in the case of the two lane structure), but the disruption to traffic and consequent user delay costs were significantly lower. The problem with these two options was the impact they would have had on the Richmond side of the bridge, necessitating the removal of trees in Hampton Court Park. Kingston Council then went one significant step further, proposing that the bridge should be widened at the same time by some 18 feet, to include new bus and cycle lanes, in a scheme costing £8-million. Bentalls were not alone in favouring this option, to promote which Edward Bentall wrote to the town's MP, the Rt Hon Norman Lamont. He wrote: 'Over the past five years following completion of the relief road with the consequent pedestrianisation of a major part of the town centre, Kingston has now become re-established as one of the most important and successful town centres from both a retailing and business point of view. As you are aware, Kingston Bridge is heavily used and with almost 50 per cent of our customers using the bridge as their entry route into the town, it is unthinkable to me that any option which does not cause the minimum of disruption should be contemplated.

'I have read the report published by the Royal Borough and fully concur with the view expressed by the Council that the best way forward would be to widen the bridge by about 7 metres. This would have the great advantage not only of bringing long-term benefit to the town but also of virtually eliminating the dreadful congestion problems with Kingston town centre and neighbouring areas which would occur if four traffic lanes were not maintained over the bridge during the refurbishment period.

'I note from the Council's report that the widening proposal is a costly option but, notwithstanding this, I am convinced that in view of the importance of Kingston Bridge to both the town centre and the surrounding area, the widening proposal is by far the best option.'

Norman Lamont replied, promising to air Bentalls' views and writing to Steven Norris MP, the Parliamentary Under-Secretary of State for Transport, to make him aware of the strength of feeling about the need for the work to be done with the minimum of disruption. The Minister met a delegation from the Council in November, 1994. In due course Government funding was agreed to the tune of £2.4-million – enough to make a start. One impediment remained. Because of the architectural significance of Kingston bridge, any major work to it requires the approval of English Heritage and although the plan calls for the facing to be removed, stored and replaced intact, they had other concerns. One was that the work would alter the width of the bridge disproportionately to its length. Another was the desire by English Heritage to preserve the spirit of the original by using bricks to construct the new section as opposed to the contemporary materials proposed, adding to the cost and the construction period of 28 months. And there, as the time of going to press, the matter rests. How the town would have appreciated the bridge that Bentalls planned!

The Royal Borough acknowledged Bentalls' contribution to the town in a framed tribute, embellished by the Great Seal of the Council and signed by the Mayor and presented to the president of Bentalls, Rowan Bentall, on the occasion of the company's 125th anniversary in 1992. It read: 'On behalf of the Council of the Royal Borough of Kingston upon Thames I wish to convey my warmest congratulations to you and to your family on the occasion of the 125th anniversary of Bentalls commencing trading in Kingston.

'The perception of your grandfather and your father before you, ensured that many years ago the store that bears your name became firmly established as a major retail outlet in this town. The contribution made to the development of Kingston is immeasurable; indeed, in the year I was born, the Mayor of Kingston (Councillor F C Digby) described your father, Leonard Hugh Bentall, as 'the man who made Kingston'.

'During the last 50 years, the third and fourth generations of the family have overseen the expansion of the Bentall Group around the south of England, thereby securing a wide trading base. We are therefore very proud that your latest development

THE MEN WHO MADE KINGSTON

The Worshipful the Mayor
Councillor David Edwards

Mayor's Parlour
Guildhall
Kingston upon Thames
Surrey KT1 1EU

Telephone 081-547 5030
          081-547 5031
Fax   081-547 6499

L E Rowan Bentall Esq D L
President
Bentalls plc

July 1992

Dear Rowan,

On behalf of the Council of the Royal Borough of Kingston upon Thames I wish to convey my warmest congratulations to you and to your family on the occasion of the 125th Anniversary of Bentalls commencing trading in Kingston.

The perception of your grandfather and your father before you, ensured that many years ago the store that bears your name became firmly established as a major retail outlet in this town. The contribution that made to the development of Kingston is immeasurable; indeed, in the year I was born, the Mayor of Kingston [Councillor F C Digby] described your father, Leonard Hugh Bentall, as "the man who made Kingston".

During the last 50 years, the third and fourth generations of the family have overseen the expansion of the Bentall Group around the south of England, thereby securing a wide trading base. We are therefore very proud that your latest development – The Bentall Centre – which is the biggest single retail scheme ever carried out in Kingston, is also the largest of its kind in Britain since the 1930's.

May Bentalls continue to prosper, and may the people of the Royal Borough continue to benefit from your success.

Yours sincerely,

David Edwards
Mayor

The framed tribute from the Royal Borough with the Great Seal

– the Bentall Centre – which is the biggest single retail scheme ever carried out in Kingston, is also the largest of its kind in Britain since the 1930s.

'May Bentalls continue to prosper, and may the people of the Royal Borough continue to benefit from your success.'

4. 'The Big Idea'

THE NURTURING OF GOOD STAFF RELATIONS

Frank Bentall established exacting standards for his staff. He himself set the example. He was a neat, precise man who recognised the virtues of personal service and who spent almost all of his time in the shop ensuring the needs of his customers were being met. His philosophy of service and reliability were the keys to the prosperity of the business.

From his staff of five he expected no less. Neatness in dress, politeness in dealing with customers and accuracy in the way they did their work, down to the meticulous wrapping and tying of parcels, were expected of them during the long hours. They started at 8am, readying the shop and the displays of merchandise for the customers, and it was 9pm and often later before the shop was tidied up ready to close. This was the pattern six days a week. But in those days worse things happened at sea, or on the land or in the mines come to that, and at least they didn't have to spend time and money on travel, most of them living literally over the shop in dormitory style accommodation. And they were fortunate in having a kindly, if demanding, employer whom they repaid with their loyalty.

THE MEN WHO MADE KINGSTON

Frank Bentall, with a number of other drapers, set a precedent in 1868 by closing his shop on Christmas Day and Boxing Day, at the time an almost unheard of concession to staff but one which other traders in the town went on to follow. A year or two later, still two decades before the regular introduction of early closing days, he and other traders closed their shops at 3pm one Wednesday in August to enable staff to watch the Kingston Town Regatta. Then, when early closing was finally introduced in 1890, which entailed finishing at 5pm on Wednesdays, he was among the first to adopt it. Those shopkeepers who failed to do so, incidentally, were subjected to demonstrations by the working folk who made up a high proportion of Kingston's population, and finally they all capitulated.

Two decades on, and with a much enlarged business employing 100 staff, working conditions at Bentalls again improved through the purchase of the former Kingston Social Club which was re-opened as the Clarence House Members' Club in September 1911. It was the initiative of Leonard Bentall, Frank's second son, who by then had begun to make his mark in the business. The Club provided not only sleeping accommodation for 50 male members of staff but recreation rooms for cards, billiards, reading and writing. There was also a small theatre with green rooms, reserved two evenings a week for female members of staff for whom in those times of stricter morals a separate entrance was provided. Behind the theatre was a miniature rifle range, no less. In the basement there was a bowling alley and outside there was a bowling green. All this in Fairfield Road, within walking distance of the store. In many of its features it expressed Leonard's belief in the value of team spirit which he acquired during his school days.

New residential and social facilities for female staff were created in 1914, just as they had been for their male colleagues three years earlier. *Clarencia*, as they were known, comprised

'The Big Idea' Chapter 4

A fancy dress ball for Bentalls' staff at their Clarence House Members' Club

four houses linked by a basement passage in Palace Road, with a maid in each to do the housework. The recreational facilities included a music room and outside there was a garden, tennis courts and a greenhouse.

It was with the interests of store staff in mind that Leonard embarked on his fundraising activities in the 1920s for the Clerks' and Drapers' schools, later the Purley and Addington Schools, and for the Roberts Marine Mansions at Bexhill-on-Sea, described in Chapter 2.

At about this time Leonard had a booklet produced giving guidelines on customer relations. In it he also wrote about the future of the business, thus: 'Our greatest need is cooperation – closer touch between management and staff, sections and individuals. I want each one to get the Big Idea of Bentalls as

'Clarencia', four houses bought in 1914 to provide residential and social facilities for female staff

an entity . . . If you would forward the interests of Bentalls together with your own, spell COOPERATION with capital letters in your brain'.

On a more prosaic level, staff rules insisted that: 'All saleswomen must wear black dresses. The wearing of jewellery (other than a ring or brooch) or coloured shoes is not permitted. Salesmen must wear black or dark grey morning or lounge coats, black or black and white ties and black boots or shoes . . . If a salesman has removed his coat he will put it on again before serving a customer, and must not on any account walk about the store with coat off.'

Such rules were commonplace in the 1920s. Far less common was the bonus scheme introduced by Bentalls in 1925. Under the scheme, an employee could contribute up to 10 per cent of his or her salary each week to which Bentalls added an annual bonus of four per cent. After five years continuous saving, an extra 10 per cent was added and the annual bonus increased to 10 per cent thereafter. A preferential scheme was then introduced for staff wanting to invest £50 or more. On this they were guaranteed an annual dividend of five per cent as well as extra dividends depending on the profitability of the store. In 1929 Bentalls introduced its own pension fund, confined at first to senior employees but later extended to all staff. Soon afterwards they became one of the first employers in the country to introduce a scheme of family allowances, which gave employees with two children under 15 an extra five shillings a week for the third child and an extra two shillings and sixpence for each additional child.

The staff welfare scheme followed a year or so later – sparked off, or so it's said, by an encounter between Leonard and three members of staff whom he saw hurrying out of a nearby shop. Astonished that they would need to shop anywhere other than at Bentalls, especially since they had the added incentive of a staff discount, he asked them to explain themselves. They replied that the shop sold cough linctus at a halfpenny a dose, which they took to ward off coughs and colds. Leonard's reaction was predictable and Bentalls' staff welfare clinic with its own matron was established in the store where it has continued, as the Occupational Health Department, ever since.

The tradition, still observed, of giving staff turkeys at Christmas began at about the same time. It started when a goose and gander were pensioned off after serving at the removals department as watchdogs, just as geese had done in ancient Rome. Leonard's wife took them under her wing and put them out to grass, the result being a healthy crop of goslings each year. Initially the gifts were reserved for senior staff but in later years everyone who had served for a year or more was presented with one personally by the head of the company. At its peak this entailed the distribution of more than 3,000 birds, the ceremony lasting over three hours. By 1949, staff numbers having fallen away during the war years, it was a more modest affair but still one which was greatly appreciated by the employees, as this extract from *Bentalls Staff News* of that year indicates.

'Over 1,400 of the Staff at Kingston, on the invitation of Mr Gerald and Mr Rowan visited the garage, a portion of which as in previous years had been transformed into one great Father Christmas parlour to receive their gifts. Each to their various section they went and at the exit stood Mr Gerald himself to wish them a Happy Christmas. Some members of the Staff may not know that Mr Gerald stood for 2½ hours shaking hands and passing on the Christmas spirit to members of the organisation. To the organisation's pensioners Mrs Gerald Bentall personally distributed the gifts and the sick were not forgotten. Sister had a busy time running round the area passing on the parcels and Christmas cheer to those who were unfortunately cast aside by illness at the festive season. In addition to the gifts, there were many who received gift warrants for long and loyal service. While the distributions were going on at Kingston, Mr Rowan was carrying out a similar ritual at Worthing, of course on a much smaller scale, but Worthing Store is growing and next year no doubt there will be more gift parcels for the 'Bentallians by the Sea.'

'Back to the Store. After Christmas a flood of letters of thanks were received from members of our organisation of all grades expressing their gratitude once again for the magnanimous gifts which they received at Christmas and reading through these letters, many of them contained fascinating and interesting paragraphs. Mr Gerald has sent a few extracts which we are pleased to reproduce, for they make very interesting reading. There were many more, but our *Staff News* is small.'

One of the extracts read as follows:

'In your speech on Christmas Eve you mentioned about the importance of small things which brought to my mind a phrase your father* had just outside his office. I was quite a young lad when I read it but I have never forgotten it. The phrase runs as follows:- "LOST. Between sunrise and sunset ONE GOLDEN HOUR – set with 60 DIAMOND MINUTES. No reward offered as it is lost for ever." This made a great impression on me.'

Leonard's belief in the importance of team spirit coupled with the provision of outstanding staff recreational facilities paved the way to a wide range of activities for staff. One of the most unusual was the series of political meetings, which continued for many years, at which local parliamentary candidates were invited to address the staff. Staff dances and concerts were regular occurrences and in 1924 the Clarence House Operatic Society was formed, giving as its maiden offering a performance of Gilbert & Sullivan's *Trial by Jury*. Sport played a key role – soccer, hockey (for men as well as women), swimming and water polo. Each June came the Clarence House sports day with a mixture of events, some serious, some less so, like the Going to Work race in which the 'husbands' lay on the ground until their 'wives' arrived with a breakfast of buns and cold water which had to be consumed before they reached the 'railway station'.

The mutual respect and affection between Leonard and the staff were never more warmly characterised than on his return with his wife after their world tour in 1937 at the 'welcome home' ball in the store described in Chapter 2. Against this background of loyalty, service and team spirit it was hardly surprising that, with the first rumblings of the Second World War, Bentalls should decide to organise its own Territorial

* Leonard Bentall

THE MEN WHO MADE KINGSTON

Army unit. Even so, for an organisation like theirs to do so was almost unique. It started life in 1936 as the 323rd (Surrey) Anti-Aircraft Company with some 300 officers and men, albeit with an outsider as commanding officer. Three years later, in August 1939, they became part of the Army proper, their first assignment being the defence of a naval base near Gosport in Hampshire with Lewis guns preserved from the First World War which had neither rear sights nor tripods. It was an inauspicious start but, with typical resourcefulness, the Bentalls men enlisted the help of the Navy and the local railway staff to manufacture gun rests from sleepers to make the guns tolerably serviceable. From Gosport they moved to Kingsworthy, near Winchester, where they were employed in road and bridge building as well as maintenance at searchlight sites in various locations. Drawn as they were from different departments, including maintenance and transport, they had many practical skills to offer. There was an ongoing contact between the men and the store, not least through regular trips by Leonard to

The Bentalls' brigade; members of the 323rd (Surrey) Anti-Aircraft Company, Royal Engineers, outside the Kingston department store in November, 1938

'The Big Idea' Chapter 4

visit the troops, and on more than one occasion Bentalls were able to supply equipment not otherwise available, including chains for the unit's vehicles when snow brought most transport to a halt.

The Company having become a Battery in 1940 when searchlight units were transferred to the Royal Artillery, it was frequently moved from place to place in the South and Midlands on such activities as fire bomb disposal and decoy work – creating dummy airfields with runway lights to distract the enemy bombers from centres of population. After three years in the UK, 323 Battery received its first overseas posting, joining the First Army in North Africa and they were among the first troops to enter Tunis when it fell in 1943. After Tunis the unit became the 323 Independent Field Searchlight Battery, recruiting from other units but still predominantly composed of Bentalls men. It transferred via tank landing craft to Taranto in Italy, thence to Naples and, in 1944, to Livorno and Fano, providing anti-aircraft support for American, Canadian, New Zealand and Indian troops in the process, frequently in the front line of action. After Italy's surrender, 323 Battery was moved to Austria and eventually demobilised. In the meantime, Rowan Bentall had served with the Eighth Army in North Africa, Sicily and Italy, landed with the initial assault in Normandy on D Day and served with the Second Army in France, Belgium and Holland until after the Battle of Arnhem.

With characteristic foresight Leonard had anticipated the difficulties wartime service might cause for the business, particularly in those jobs which were considered to be for men only – driving delivery vans, for example. He therefore decided to establish in advance a reserve of *women* drivers, a highly innovative step at a time when few women drove even cars. When war was declared, Bentalls' Women's Auxiliary Driving Unit was ready to spring into action, kitted out in green coats, hats, dresses and ties, driving everything from small vans to 30cwt delivery vehicles.

With so many of their colleagues called to arms (two years after the war began, of the original staff of 2,400 only 700 remained), life for those remaining was not easy. However, among the store's customers there were many women who willingly volunteered their services to work full or part-time. There were constant reminders of their colleagues in the Forces, through efforts like the Bentall Hurricane Fund, which raised the £5,000 necessary to give the RAF a new fighter (Leonard, as he promised he would, doubling the £2,500 raised by the staff). Bentalls made an indirect contribution to the production of Hurricanes by enabling its manufacturers, Hawkers, who were based in Kingston, to use large sections of the store for the storage of aircraft parts, tool making and other activities.

On August Bank Holiday, 1940, Leonard declared a day of National Service, and told the staff: 'It is to be a matter of honour for each one of us personally to dedicate ourselves to some service for our country on this day'.

A fortnight after the day of National Service, staff had their first real taste of war damage. On the night of 17 August, 1940, a bomb fell on the store, one of the first to fall on London, incidentally, smashing through the show bungalow on the roof of the store and exploding in the piano department on the second floor, destroying nearly 50 instruments.

The war over and with it the reign of Leonard Bentall, who died in 1942, his son Gerald faced the dilemma of staff returning to do jobs which others had done for them in their absence. Like father, like son, he had anticipated the problem and had had questionnaires sent to every employee serving in the Forces shortly before demobilisation, asking if they planned to return and, if so, in what capacity. As they returned, each was interviewed individually and given a refresher course on the store and all the changes that had taken place during the war, culminating in a written exam to determine their suitability for future employment. Those with housing or other difficulties were given sympathetic treatment.

In 1946 Bentalls became a public company, a move into which it was forced by penal duties following Leonard's death. With Gerald Bentall now at the helm and his younger brother, Rowan, assisting him in the role of Merchandise Director, the next decade saw some important developments from the staffing point of view. One was the addition of 'outside' staffs through Bentalls' acquisition of independent drapery businesses in Worthing and Ealing in 1947 and 1950. They were the beginnings of the chain of Bentalls' branch stores in the South East. A second was the introduction of a training scheme for university graduates designed to lead to management opportunities in due course. A third was the opening of new facilities, the provision of which had been interrupted by the war, in the shape of a large mansion with 10 acres of grounds in West Molesey. It opened in 1948 as the Sports and Social Club. The following year it inaugurated the annual staff Sunday outing to the Isle of Wight, which continued until comparatively recently, when 1,200 Bentalls employees travelled in two special trains via Portsmouth to Ryde and back. The following year saw a revival of the sports days, re-named Family Days, for 4,000 staff and their families at the new West Molesey premises.

Two other events of significance to staff present and past happened at about the same time. One was the establishment of a General Staff Council, forerunner of today's Joint Consultative Committees and Central Joint Council, giving employees a say in decision-making, and the other was the formation of the Old Bentallians' Association for former employees, which is still in being. Then, in 1951, completing,

THE MEN WHO MADE KINGSTON

The Clarence House river party of 1910, forerunner of many subsequent staff outings

for the time being, a significant post-war investment by Bentalls in its staff, came the opening in the store of a new staff restaurant, providing food at cost price and facilities for relaxation, costing £50,000.

Bentalls have always been aware of the need to strike a balance between meeting the needs of their customers and creating decent working conditions for their staff. They were in the van of moves to reduce shop workers' hours in Kingston back in 1890. They were the first store in the UK to introduce late night Friday shopping in 1946. And they were one of the first stores to introduce a five day working week in 1961. Nine years later, whilst retaining the five day working week for staff, they began six day trading. In the early 1980s, late night shopping was re-introduced, the Kingston store remaining open until 9pm on Fridays, subsequently changed to Thursdays, a much more popular evening.

Then, as recently as June 1995, the gradual evolution in shopping and leisure habits in the UK brought Sunday trading

'The Big Idea' Chapter 4

to Kingston and the store began trading seven days a week. Acknowledging the extra demands made on staff and management by this significant expansion of trading hours, the directors introduced a package of remuneration and time off to take this into account. With it came the affirmation that the support and understanding of the staff were crucial to Bentalls' continuing success.

Staff loyalty has been one of the great strengths of Bentalls, a good guide being length of service. The 1972 annual report recorded the fifth member of staff to record 50 years' service and the retirement of two other staff members, one after 44 years and the other after 47. It also reported that the number of staff working full time with over 25 years' service totalled 140*. Significantly, Rowan Bentall, the then Chairman, wrote of the impending Industrial Relations Act and Code of Practice that they 'will have little effect on our staff relations policy as we are already either applying the principles of the Code or have taken the necessary steps to introduce the remainder'.

Similarly, with the introduction of the Social Security Act 1973, requiring that arrangements should be made for employees to receive an earnings-related pension in addition to the State pension, Bentalls were able to achieve recognition for their own Superannuation Fund for all executive staff set up 45 years earlier. This was established for buyers, managers and senior staff with the object of providing pensions from the age of 65.

There was a strengthening of staff training facilities during

* More than 20 years on, the 1993 edition of the 'Old Bentallians' News' recorded the current crop of retirees one of whom had completed 50 years, a second 46 years, a third 44 years, and six more than 30 years' service. By 1995, the number of members of staff awarded gold watches for 25 years service exceeded 600. By the same date, 144 had served for over 40 years and 17 for over 50 years.

83

1973. In addition to in-store training, student staff were encouraged to acquire further qualifications by means of day release. That year, 56 Bentalls students qualified in their City & Guilds and College of Distributive Trades final examinations and a Bentalls' Student of the Year cup was inaugurated. If it was intended as an incentive, it was certainly successful; by 1977 the number of youngsters embarking on training schemes had more than doubled to 116. The sports ground in West Molesey, opened in 1948 and the scene of countless Family Days and other events, was sold in 1974 for housing development – a sign of the times in which organisations of the size of Bentalls could no longer afford the luxury of such facilities, and the fact that with the growing influence of television their popularity had gradually diminished. In its place, Bentalls opened a well appointed staff club immediately opposite the store, through which a range of sports and social activities continued to be provided.

Staff participation had long been a strong point of the company so much so that when the Bullock Report appeared in 1977 with its recommendations for worker participation, there were already 15 Joint Consultative Committees within the organisation, and Bentalls viewed the new proposals with concern. As the Chairman, Rowan Bentall, expressed it at the time: 'We accept the principle of worker participation but think this should grow from roots established within the business and not [be] applied from above by national edict which has no consideration for the individual circumstances within a company'.

The Profit Sharing Share Scheme introduced in the 1978 Finance Act with the aim of creating employee shareholders was duly adopted by the Bentalls management. However, in 1983, Rowan's eldest son, Edward, having succeeded to the chairmanship, Bentalls' employees were among the first to be offered the opportunity to take advantage of a savings-related share option scheme. It was made available to those with three or more years' service. They were required to enter into a regular savings contract for National Savings or with a building society; the sums saved, plus the tax-free bonus on them, provided the monies with which to subscribe for shares in Bentalls.

Bentalls had produced its own staff news-sheet at regular intervals for a number of years when, in 1986, it decided to introduce a more comprehensive version aimed at improving the flow of information between management and staff, increasing staff knowledge about the variety of different jobs their colleagues performed and enhancing a sense of satisfaction in their achievements. Professionally written and designed, *Bentalls Bulletin* appeared twice a year and carried news and features about Kingston and all the branch stores, about new trends in marketing and other developments of interest, not least the new Bentall Centre development which had been approved in principle shortly before the first issue appeared. *The Bulletin* continued to be published twice a year until it ceased publication in 1992, a victim of the recession.

In 1988, a year before the Government decided to 'blow the froth off' consumer spending (and before the recession did the job for them) Bentalls were able to record a £1-million increase in pre-tax profits to nearly £5-million. With the awareness of the importance of involving staff in the continuing (and, as it then seemed to almost all sectors of the economy, unending) success of the business, Bentalls greatly increased the number of executives on performance-related incentive payments and extended the system of direct sales commission to almost all sales staff.

Four years later, following three years of adverse trading conditions and the first financial loss in the company's history,

85

the *Bentalls Bulletin* was not the only redundancy as the organisation was re-structured to meet the new circumstances in which Bentalls found themselves. In common with the majority of organisations which had weathered the recession successfully, Bentalls had been obliged to look carefully at their staffing levels. By the beginning of 1995, staff numbers stood at just over 1,100,* the lowest for many years, though with the advent of seven day trading it is likely to rise again before long.

Rowan Bentall gave rich expression to the contribution made by the staff to the success of Bentalls in his introduction to *My Store of Memories* which he dedicated to them. He wrote: 'For while new buildings go up, innovations introduced, or exciting promotions launched – all commanding the headlines of their day – the staff continue their efforts to make our stores the great emporiums that they are; ticket-writers carry on ticket-writing, delivery men carry on delivering, cleaners carry on cleaning, buyers carry on buying. Some of them never see the limelight, others have their brief moment on the stage before returning once more to the wings. But most of them have their tales to tell and all of them are united in a wonderful spirit which has been the lynch-pin of the fortunes of Bentalls.'

---

* FTE, or full-time staff equivalent. The actual number of individuals employed is about 1,600.

5. 'Our Store, Your Store'

CARING FOR THE CUSTOMERS

From the very outset, Frank Bentall recognised the importance of providing customers with a personal service of the highest quality. A customer profile in those early days would have daunted a man of lesser resolution. As described in Chapter 3, families of nine or more were not unusual and earnings of three pounds and five shillings a week the norm. Most of Frank Bentall's customers were in a similar situation – large families and small incomes. Yet from such unpromising beginnings did the Bentalls' enterprise expand and prosper.

The Bentalls' style was established in Frank's very first advertisement on acquiring the business. Whereas his predecessor, James Hatt, 'begged to inform his patrons' that he was relinquishing the business and 'trusts that those favours so liberally bestowed on him during the last 20 years may be continued to his successor', Frank was less obsequious and more direct. Having bought Mr Hatt's entire stock, he announced he was offering it for sale 'at greatly reduced prices in order to effect a speedy clearance'. A week later he was telling his customers that, in addition to clearing what remained of Mr Hatt's stock, he had bought his own merchandise for cash at 'much below the market value' and this was also on offer at attractive prices. The Bentalls philosophy of buying well, advertising effectively and selling competitively was born.

It was soon followed by a steady expansion in the range of goods on offer, gradually taking it out of the narrow confines of the drapery trade into new areas. First came millinery, hosiery, fashion goods and underwear, coupled with a dressmaking department. Then followed carpets and matting. Next came a department for mourning wear. This in turn provided opportunities for enhancing the company's reputation for good service, and what today would be called expanding the customer base, since orders for mourning wear could be accepted at any time of day or night and often entailed measuring up the whole family for the appropriate clothes.

The millinery department c1929

The expansion in merchandise was facilitated by the expansion of the shop as, one by one, adjoining premises were acquired and adapted. By 1904, 37 years after Frank had acquired it, it was no longer recognisable as a shop but as a small department store, stretching from Clarence Street round the corner into Wood Street. It boasted floor-to-ceiling plate glass windows, a large staircase to the upper floors, and more departments – boots and shoes, fancy goods, haberdashery, curtains and soft furnishings – with extensive staff accommodation at the top of the building and, in the basement, sections for receiving goods and marking them off, sorting and dispatch.

The competitive pricing of goods continued to be a major plank in Bentalls policy. In a newspaper article featuring the newly enlarged store in May 1904, Leonard Bentall is quoted as saying: 'We buy everything for cash and therefore we get special discounts and are able to supply goods at particularly low figures'. But now this policy was augmented by an idea Leonard Bentall imported from the USA, the guarantee that if any purchase proved unsatisfactory Bentalls would refund the purchase price or supply an alternative article in its place. And, as if this were not enough incentive, Bentalls equipped themselves with a fleet of horse-drawn vans and proceeded to offer a free delivery service to any customers within a 20-mile radius.

By 1907, further expansions of the premises led to yet more new departments in what was now being promoted as 'the finest store and shopping centre to be found in Surrey'. They included china and glass, toilet ware, stationery, silver and silver plate, toys and games, leather goods, luggage, beds and bedding. In their advertisements they made a feature of the fittings and decorations of the store and provided attendants to show the customers round, with a guarantee that they would be under no pressure to buy anything. Features that were pointed out to them on these guided tours were the extensive use of electric lighting (still something of a novelty in the early years of the century) and the spectacular pneumatic cash system. This was the first installation by the Lamson Tube Company and the ceiling mounted arrangement of wires along which metal tubes were propelled at high speed from cash point to counter and back was a great attraction for young and old.

Then there were the Bentalls sales, then as now among the highlights on the customer calendar. In 1907 it was called a Red Letter Week and on offer were teddy bears at 5s 11½d, alarm clocks at 1s 11¾d, 'fine white toilet pails' at 1s 10¾d and a 54-piece semi-porcelain dinner service, which normally retailed at £1 3s 6d, on sale at 11s 9d. (One marvels, 25 years after decimalisation and the pocket calculator, at how customers and staff coped with the monetary system.) Bentalls sales have become an institution and over the years have been seen not only as an opportunity to generate sales during otherwise quiet periods and of moving slow lines but also of offering some quite exceptional bargains as a way of saying 'thank you' to their customers. It started in the time of Frank Bentall when at the conclusion of his Red Letter Weeks came the Blue Cross Day. On the last Friday, Frank walked round the store and marked with a blue cross anything he particularly wanted to dispose of. The following day they were on offer at half the original sale price. Other department store groups have since adopted the idea, but Frank Bentall was its instigator and it continues to be a feature of winter and summer sales at Kingston and Bentalls' branch stores.

The same period witnessed the beginnings of Bentalls' mail order business. Pattern books were despatched to customers from the Cotton and Wool Dress Department on request, the orders being received for the company's workrooms by post or, from the more affluent, by telephone, or even, when the store was closed, via the night watchmen, thus providing a round-the-clock ordering service. This was just the beginning. Within two or three years, Bentalls were emulating the biggest department stores and producing their own 350-page mail order catalogue which, as well as bringing in new business, was a means of advertising the store to an ever wider audience.

In 1907, too, came the concept of providing catering facilities for the customers, marked by the opening of the lavish, Moorish tea rooms, forerunners of the in-store restaurants of later years. Although not new to department stores in London, this represented something of a culture shock for the citizens of Kingston, one to which they responded with enthusiasm, not least because the entrance doors opened automatically as soon as someone stepped on the mat in front of them – the so-called 'Sesame doors'.

These were among the most innovative times in Bentalls' history. In 1910 came the first of the immensely successful special promotions – in this case an 'All British Show' which ran for a week and which had as its logo a Union Jack and the figure of John Bull and his bulldog. Not only were all the goods on offer of British manufacture, in many cases the craftsmen who made them came to the store to demonstrate how they were produced. There were hatmakers from Luton, bootmakers from Northampton, matmakers from Norfolk and brushmakers from London.

Frank Bentall having retired in 1909 and the name having changed soon afterwards simply to Bentalls, the store took another surge forward in 1919 when the Clarence Arms was acquired, paving the way for an unbroken frontage along Clarence Street. It led to the construction of a new façade in Portland stone and the accolade 'Greater London's greatest store' bestowed on it by the *Surrey Comet*, the opening of a large and impressive millinery department, departments for new and second-hand furniture, and an extended restaurant. Leonard

Bentall's lifelong fascination with *gizmos* was given free rein. There were synchronomes (electric clocks in each department run from a master clock on the ground floor), Measuregraphs (which told an assistant the price of a piece of material and where to cut it to the required length) and the latest Lamson tube development, the Belt Desk Automatic Power Control Pneumatic Tube System.

Year by year, extension followed extension. In 1924 the size of the china and glass department was doubled, the boot and shoe department restyled, the silk department resited and the men's department expanded to include a 'Twentieth Century' man's shop. Two years later, the store's golden jubilee was marked by the opening of the splendid Tudor Restaurant with period chandeliers, murals depicting scenes from Kingston's history painted by Hermon Cawthra, stained glass windows and, somewhat incongruously, a soda fountain. Next came the new covered car park immediately opposite the store to accommodate 450 vehicles, with a workshop for repairing customers' cars. Even though these were the comparatively early days of car ownership and there was not a little scepticism in the town about the car park's chances of success, it became necessary to introduce a season ticket scheme in order to guarantee customers a space. Bentalls added a car showroom a few years later and were in the business of selling cars up until the early 1990s.

In 1929, Bentalls converted an engineering works which they acquired a short distance from the store into a furniture depository; in the same year another new customer service was provided in-store – a sub post office. In what is a common enough development now, but rare in the '20s, the Post Office agreed to the Clarence Street office being re-located in non-GPO property. A year later, the provision of alcoholic drinks in the Tudor restaurant became available – not without considerable opposition from an unholy alliance between the town's licensed victuallers and local temperance workers. Little wonder there was opposition. By this time the restaurant was serving up to 900 lunches and 1,500 teas daily as well as catering for private parties of up to 500. The Free Church Council were concerned that boys from the nearby Kingston Grammar School who sometimes lunched in the restaurant would be 'in the midst of folk who were drinking, and on every table, even if there were not modicums of strong drink, there would be wine lists' . . . As for the waitresses 'it would be very unfortunate that they should be trained and used in the dispensing and handling of strong drink'. The proceedings lasted four hours before the licensing justices reached their decision to agree to Bentalls' request.

Meanwhile, things were moving apace towards Leonard Bentall's design for a 'superstore', in terms of the acquisition of land and buildings, the commissioning of the architect – Maurice Webb of Sir Aston Webb and Sons – and the preliminary construction work. The store which was to serve generations of customers for 60 years until the middle of the present decade was finally completed in 1935 though sections were phased in during the preceding three or four years. The Wood Street extension, for example, opened its doors – and the eyes of its customers – in November 1931. An eye opener it truly was. The large, semi circular vestibule was designed in consultation with a famous French designer, Ferdinand Chanut, with floodlighting, impressive showcases and two overhead clocks giving the time of day and lighting up time respectively*. Two sets of doors led into the store proper which, as contemporary drawings show, bore striking resemblance to the atrium of the new Bentall Centre and was in every sense ahead of its time.

* The Chanut vestibule has been preserved in the Bentall Centre.

Artist's impression of the Bentalls fleet of vans outside the Wood Street frontage of the Kingston store in the 1930s

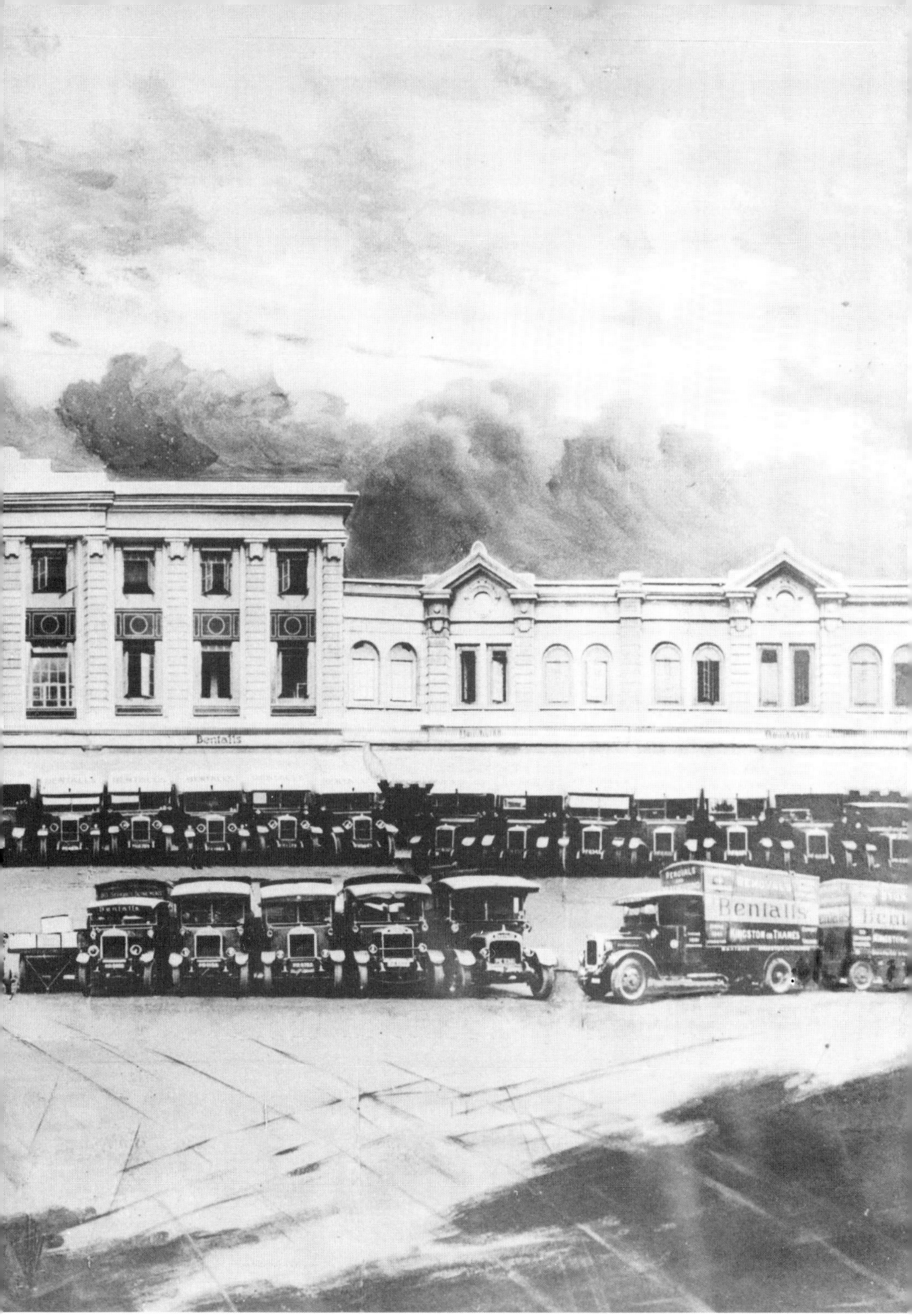
Bentalls
Bentalls

On either side were escalators to take customers up three floors to the top of the store. Popular in the USA, escalators were sufficiently novel over here for it to be necessary to provide staff as well as customers with instruction in how to use them – in the form of a repeated message on a gramophone.

A smaller part of the Wood Street section was completed a year later. This had a large new room, the mannequin hall, which also served as an extension to the restaurant. The new section also included Bentalls' first food hall as well as a wine and spirits department and yet another innovation, a ladies' hairdressing salon. The following year, the acquisition of White's mineral water factory which backed on to the Wood Street premises brought further improvements, including the resiting of the small factory where Bentalls made their own furniture, as well as an extended upholstery and repair section. It facilitated the opening of a new customer entrance in Fife Road – an event in itself, since the doors were operated automatically by photoelectric cells for the particular benefit of ladies with prams, and just inside was a pram park with an attendant as well as a trained nurse, a boon to mums for years to come.

The Escalator Hall, as it became known, was the setting for an experiment, the consequences of which have become a key part of retailing life, especially food retailing, today. The Advertising Exhibition in London in 1933 featured 'The Shop of 1950 – the Packeteria'. Bentalls bought the exhibition lock, stock and barrel and installed it in the new hall. Everything in it was pre-packed and price marked. The customer was given a tray which was pushed on rails. At the exit, an assistant assessed value and took the money. Self-service had arrived. The irony was that the concept was totally alien to the Bentall policy of customer service. Though it was not adopted by them, two decades later retailers began using it as a way of life with which nowadays we are only too familiar.

'Our Store, Your Store' Chapter 5

Artist's impression of the Escalator Hall in the 1935 store, to which the atrium in the new Bentall Centire bears some striking similarities

THE MEN WHO MADE KINGSTON

The Packeteria – 'the shop of 1950'

The re-built store opened in 1935 to a fanfare of trumpets. Its most notable feature was the superb frontage designed in the style of Hampton Court Palace and known as the Aston Webb façade, retained as part of the Bentall Centre of the 1990s. There were yet more new or enlarged departments – gentlemen's outfitting, art needlework and fancy goods, ladies' footwear and model millinery and a very modern gentlemen's hairdressing salon. There were special promotions of various kinds, the most innovative being the Radio-Bentalls exhibition, based on the concept of Radiolympia. The days of the old crystal sets and cat's whisker wireless were at an end. Radio as we know it today had arrived and Bentalls were among the first to give their customers the benefits of the new technology, which in that pre-TV era was the prime means of mass entertainment. Radio-Bentalls was a smash hit and brought people flocking to the new store. One of the attractions was a machine which allowed them to record their voice on disc for 6d; another was the succession of well-known personalities from the world of entertainment who visited the exhibition during its two-week run.

By this time Bentalls' customers were used to the concept of special promotions. The 1930s had brought the former publicity director of Gamages, Eric Fleming, on to the Kingston staff. Leonard Bentall's penchant for publicity coupled with Fleming's skills were a potent combination. If the idea of mannequin displays and bouncy baby competitions sound old hat, their effectiveness can be judged from the fact that the former attracted twice-daily audiences of more than 500 and the latter entries of as many as 3,000. A world food exhibition of 1933 had official government stands for Australia, New Zealand and South Africa, backed up by cooking demonstrations and followed by food lectures. In the same year there was a sewing exhibition, embellished by the presence of the reigning Lancashire Cotton Queen.

The idea of visiting celebrities was destined to become a part of Bentalls' culture. They extended to most departments, sports equipment in particular, as well as the restaurant where a series of well-known bands and singers made appearances, and the gardening section where the Percy Thrower of the day, C H Middleton of Surrey County Council's parks and gardens department who broadcast regularly on the BBC, gave occasional talks on Saturday mornings to capacity audiences. One of the earliest guest appearances was that of Sir Malcolm Cambell's world land speed record beating *Bluebird* in 1932. The following year, the Escalator Hall became a film set on which Ivor Novello and several leading actresses of the day appeared. This event prompted Eric Fleming to create a semi permanent film set with resident camera operators and make up artist where customers could take short screen tests at 2s 6d a throw.

Bentalls were expanding into quite new territory during this same period. Selling as they did virtually everything necessary to furnish a home, it was a logical step to create their own building department. In the 1930s they won a contract to build over 100 houses in Norbiton for Kingston Corporation. They also built the new headquarters for the Steadfast Sea Cadets with which Leonard Bentall was so closely associated. Two of their most celebrated achievements were the modernisation and redecoration of the Thirlmere Hotel at Hindhead, opened by the former Prime Minister David Lloyd George, and extensive work at Buxted Park, near Uckfield, for a close friend of Queen Mary. The department also built timber-framed bungalows which, at £175 each, were in great demand among Bentalls' customers as retirement homes, many of which were erected by Bentalls' workmen on the south coast. It was the show bungalow, erected on the roof of the store for demonstration purposes (it was also a showcase for furnishing displays in the days when it was possible to furnish a three-bedroomed house from top to bottom for £100), which bore the brunt of the bomb which fell on Bentalls on 17 August 1940. The building department was discontinued after the war but an associated development of the same vintage, the estate agency, continues to this day, not only for the sale of houses but also for property lettings.

Back at the store, and another idea to attract customers was being put to the acid test. Christmas was traditionally reserved for some of Bentalls' ambitious promotions and in the early '30s it was decided to introduce a circus, complete with elephant, lion and other animals. In the event, the logistics of staging an event of this nature proved overwhelming and it was abandoned after three or four years. One of the most diverting of a series of incidents occurred when the elephant, hired from Chessington Zoo and paraded through Kingston to advertise Bentalls' latest attraction, backed into the entrance of another store and the inevitable happened. The place had to be closed for over half an hour before mopping-up operations were completed.

Of all the special events, there was nothing to compare with the arrival in the store in the summer of 1937 of a diminutive Swedish girl named Anita Kittner, at least in the opinion of Rowan Bentall, who wrote in *My Store of Memories*: 'The forte of Miss Kittner, a young Swedish woman, was to dive from a great height into a small pool of water, an act she performed in the escalator hall twice daily for a fortnight – once in the morning and once in the afternoon. The balconies of the upper floors were as packed as the ground floor on every occasion. In bathing costume and hat, and to the accompaniment of music, Miss Kittner climbed up a ladder held by struts until she reached the top of the well, her head nearly touching the glass roof. As the music stopped and customers held their breath she would take off her shoes and throw them down. Then she would climb on all fours out along a diving board and performed a handstand at the end of it. And finally, with a blood-curdling scream she leapt. Apart from the basic danger of this feat – the likelihood of sudden death – there were one or two minor complications. As Miss Kittner plunged 63 feet into the tank of water she put tremendous pressure on the floor so that we decided to shore up the ceiling of the lower ground floor beneath. On a more personal level there was great pressure exerted on her costume – so much so that on one occasion it split in two. No doubt to the disappointment of some, one of our electricians, Mr Tom Bliss, was nearby to snatch up a towel and wrap it round her . . . After her final dive a member of the staff stepped forward and presented her with a bouquet of flowers – the biggest I think I have ever seen. It was nearly as tall as the girl herself. This was a typically warm-hearted and spontaneous gesture by the staff. None of the directors had any hand in it and I did not wish to pry by asking who had been the instigator.'

Two years later Anita Kittner was invited back to take part in a Hollywood Fair, conceived by Leonard as an antidote to the post Depression blues that seemed to be engulfing the county in much the same way as the lack of business confidence persisted for some time after the 1990s Recession had ended.

The centrepiece was a re-creation of part of the California coast and it was notable as the first occasion on which Max Factor cosmetics were on special display. There was a cabaret, a marionette show, appearances by well-known sports personalities and, of more practical benefit, lectures on mothercraft, and for a few brave spirits, fathercraft as well, Bentalls having provided a permanent space in the store for use by the Mothercraft Training Society. And there was also Anita Kittner to thrill the crowds once more, though not for very much longer; she was killed during a performance elsewhere not long afterwards, to the profound distress of Bentalls and many of their customers.

Bentalls did their best to cater for their customers during the war years when much of their stock in trade became increasingly difficult to come by. The absence of over 800 male employees was a major handicap, though there was a ready response from local housewives to Bentalls' advertisement for part-time staff and, with characteristic foresight, Leonard had established a corps of women delivery drivers shortly before the outbreak of hostilities. Even so within a couple of years only 700 of the original staff of 2,400 remained in the store. Bentalls' buyers bought how and where they could and in the largest quantities available, even at the risk of being left with stock on their hands. That probability was never greater than with a consignment of a million and a half Chinese hairnets yet they were all sold within a very short space of time.

It was just after the war that Bentalls began to expand their customer base with the acquisition of stores outside Kingston. First, in 1947, almost by accident, came the store in Worthing, originally established by a cousin of Frank Bentall. It seems the Worthing branch of the family were on the point of selling up to Debenhams. A chance remark by someone involved in the negotiations found its way to Kingston where the two brothers, Gerald and Rowan, successfully strove to keep it in the family. Three years later came the store in Ealing. Since then, stores have been acquired or built at the rate of one a decade – Tunbridge Wells in the '60s, Bracknell in the '70s, Tonbridge in the '80s and Lakeside (Thurrock) in the '90s – and their progress, including that of the abortive venture at Chatham in 1979 and the more recent disposal of Tunbridge Wells, is covered in the next chapter.

At Kingston, the immediate post war years were devoted to re-staffing and re-stocking the store and resuming the promotional activities now, sadly, without the enthusiasm of Leonard, who died in 1942, or the expertise of Eric Fleming, who left the store four years later. The USA having proved a fruitful source of inspiration in the past, Rowan Bentall embarked on a six-week trip to the USA in 1947, travelling 12,000 miles and visiting 38 stores including Macys, Marshall Field, Saks, Fifth Avenue, Sears Roebuck and Bloomingdales. He recorded his impressions in a 37 page booklet entitled *My American Tour* for private circulation among colleagues and friends in which he concluded: 'America, without coupons, rationing, queues, austerity and utility standards, with few restrictions and no recent experience of blitzes, no war and death at her doorstep, is cheerful, colourful, enterprising, ingenious, self-confident. On the whole, the women are smartly dressed, fashion conscious, making great emphasis on matching accessories. Average homes neatly and tastefully furnished, well-equipped kitchens with every conceivable gadget and labour-saving device, in which they take great pride. Food plentiful; waste deplorable. In the big cities, especially in the East, the speed of living, noise, size and bustle is staggering to the newcomer. Many stores have become huge machines, tending to lose the human touch; the precious and all-important possession of courtesy is often sadly lacking. May we never fail to guard and foster this great attribute. There is no place like Bentalls, and I was glad to get back to England.'

Rowan brought back a host of ideas from across the Atlantic which were to prove valuable to the business in the years that followed, though in light of some of his observations it was not surprising that the first major promotion after his return was 'We Believe in England' in 1948. This was much more than a repeat of the 'All British Show' of 1910; over and above the displays and demonstrations of British made goods, Bentalls sent out 20,000 individually signed letters to companies all over the country urging them to look to the future with confidence and offering each of them 2,000 stickers carrying the Union Jack and the slogan 'We Believe in England'. The response was remarkable and some 11-million stickers were distributed. It was an initiative of which Leonard would have been proud.

Simultaneously, Bentalls created an export shop within the store to further promote the sale of British goods free of purchase tax. It proved highly successful and owed much of its initial popularity to the fact that in this Olympic Games year 2,000 athletes from all over the world were camped nearby in Richmond Park for several weeks. A Bentalls' car provided a shuttle service for them to and from the store where the display windows echoed the Olympic theme.

Closer to home, Bentalls were approached by Charterhouse to supply their uniform requirements and run a school shop. The operation was complicated by the fact that the service also included household goods, laundry, shoes, hairdressing and a tuck shop – not quite Bentalls' scene, though it had its compensations when a boy called Peter May, destined to become one of England's finest batsmen, was scoring centuries for his school. In the event, the venture was abandoned by mutual consent after two or three years.

Bentalls were on much surer ground with their newly-launched children's book weeks during which authors visited the store not just to sign autographs but to give talks about their craft. They soon blossomed into regular book exhibitions for customers of all ages, the first of which took place in 1952 when no fewer than 30 publishers took stands and there were personal appearances by Hammond Innes, Wolf Mankowitz and L A G Strong. The names of other authors to visit the store in subsequent years are listed in Chapter 3.

Politics became an unlikely vehicle for promoting the store when it was decided to erect a huge results board on the outside of the building for the 1950 General Election, years before television began to satisfy the public demand to know the results as soon as they came in. Later the same year, in conjunction with the Metropolitan Police, Bentalls staged a crime prevention exhibition with a chamber of horrors including such niceties as a letter from Jack the Ripper and a guest appearance by the first 'radio cop', PC49 Brian Reece. This was followed by a nylon exhibition demonstrating the processing, manufacture and uses of the material that was to revolutionise the clothing industry. Rowan Bentall had visited the British Nylon Spinners factory to see it at first hand, the first retailer to do so. It had the added long term benefit of guaranteeing Bentalls' supplies of new lines as they were produced – shirts, lingerie, tennis rackets, golf bags, umbrellas and so on. A few years later, at the 1955 Ideal Homes Exhibition, Bentalls were to exhibit a Nylons Shop which was visited by HRH the Queen and the Duke of Edinburgh.

In the wake of the short-lived Christmas circuses now came an innovation which won the hearts and minds of many of Bentalls' customers, the creation of 'Jimminy Jingle'. Inspired by Marshall Field's 'Mr Holly', Jimminy Jingle was a 38ft high model of a bearded figure wearing a battered top hat and polka dot trousers, hoisted by crane on to the roof of the store for the festive season. Its installation was preceded by a fancy dress procession around the town. The procession in 1950 in which 500 members of Bentalls' staff took part, together with Japanese girls carrying lanterns, boys from the Gordon Homes on

HRH the Queen at the Nylons Shop in 1955; Gerald Bentall is on the left

'Our Store, Your Store' Chapter 5

HRH Queen Mary visiting the store in 1951; Rowan Bentall is on her left

hobby-horses, models of reindeer and the Central Band of the RAF, was shown on children's television by the BBC.

Another Christmas initiative from the same period which was to have pleasant repercussions was Bentalls' agreement to allow ladies living in Grace and Favour apartments in Hampton Court Palace to make table decorations and sell them through the store to raise funds for the nearby Royal Cambridge Home for Soldiers' Widows of which Queen Mary was patron. The guiding spirit, a Mrs Barbara Brooke, later offered Bentalls some Victorian costumes for exhibitions – again to raise money for the Home. The event having been arranged, Bentalls received the news that the Home's patron wished to visit the exhibition. It was to be the first of several Royal visits to the store, Queen Mary making a great hit with staff and customers.

Two other charities received Bentalls' support around the

same time. One was the West Sussex Association for the Care of Cripples, for which an exhibition of English homes through the ages was staged in the store and attended by the Duke and Duchess of Norfolk. The other was in aid of the Soldiers', Sailors' and Airmens' Families Association. For this, the eight cylinder supercharged Mercedes Benz used by Hermann Goering was on show in Bentalls' garage.

One of the most successful promotions in the store's history had its beginnings in 1951 with a display of wedding accessories and new home furnishings. The next year it had been transformed into the June Bride promotion which demonstrated that Bentalls could provide a comprehensive service, from clothes, furniture and household goods to catering, honeymoon and the bridal gown. The key to the success of the scheme was nominating an actual bride-to-be. As luck would have it, two young employees were planning to marry early in June – on a combined income of £13 a week. Producers of appropriate goods were approached and invited to be involved in the June Bride; 107 agreed, contributing gifts worth over £2,300. Such was the attendant publicity that some 5,000 people turned out to watch the couple make their way to Kingston Parish Church for the wedding travelling in a landau with four greys, grey toppered coachman and red-coated postilion. The reception was held in the store's Normandie restaurant. Even the wedding cake was made by Bentalls.

Bentalls' on-going love affair with new technology manifested itself in 1955 with another radio exhibition, coupled this time with TV and opened by a famous announcer – and regular Bentalls customer – Sylvia Peters. Commercial television was in its first flush and with typical foresight Rowan Bentall, now deputy chairman, appointed staff to monitor programmes during the day and evening in order to identify opportunities for special promotions in the store. An even more ambitious

'Our Store, Your Store' Chapter 5

An Italy in Kingston window display

exhibition followed a year later, opened by the singer Edmund Hockridge, which had its own television studio from which live programmes on fashion, make-up and shopping were relayed throughout the store. Also on show were an underwater television camera and a television telephone which enabled the callers to see one another as they were speaking. Some years later, in 1963 to be precise, Bentalls became the first store in Europe to display colour TV, and the department continues to be one of the most successful and innovative.

This was also the time of the beginning of a long and highly successful series of promotions introducing customers to the merchandise of other European countries. The first, and perhaps most successful, was Italy in Kingston in 1955. In preparation for the event, the store's buyers toured Italy and Rowan Bentall visited Venice where he arranged the purchase of a 36 ft long gondola with the Chamber of Commerce and persuaded a local sculptor to recreate his studio in the store for the two weeks of the exhibition. The event was opened by the Italian Ambassador in London, Count Vittorio Zoppi, in company with John Boyd-Carpenter (the local MP), the Italian born wife of Peter Thornycroft, then president of the Board of Trade, and Charles (now Lord) Forte in his capacity as president of the Anglo-Italian Chamber of Commerce. The displays colourfully arranged in the grand setting of the escalator hall were a minor sensation and among the many features was the banner awarded to the winner of the annual bareback horse race in Siena which had never before been allowed out of the town, a 1904 Fiat and the Formula 1 grand prix Maserati in which Roy Salvadori had won at Goodwood the previous week. An accompanying *concours d'élégance* was judged by Mike Hawthorn (who died in a road accident not long afterwards), Pat Moss and the pre-war driver Kaye Don, the prizes being presented by the actress Phyllis Calvert. Not surprisingly, the event achieved extensive publicity that extended worldwide and made a lasting impression on those customers who had the good fortune to visit it. There was some useful post-exhibition publicity, too, following Rowan's advertisement in the *Daily Telegraph* offering a surplus gondola for sale. The *Daily Express* picked up the story, the improbable outcome being that an American magnesium magnate read about it whilst breakfasting in Stockholm and bought it for the Miami Yacht Club, of which he happened to be president.

Italy came to Kingston again in 1970, this time in the guise of Italia Romantica, complete with a 10 ft wide colour copy of Leonardo's Last Supper (later donated to Kingston Parish Church where it may still be seen) and an 8 ft statue of Michelangelo's statue of David made in Florence for the event, albeit complete with fig leaf in deference to English sensibilities. In the intervening years there had been the American Fair of 1960,

Watercolour by Bert Hawes of the Bentalls depository exhibited in the architectural section of the Royal Academy in 1936

The Bentall Centre during construction

Her Majesty the Queen talking to Rowan Bentall during her visit to Kingston in 1992

Part of the interior of the Kingston store soon after its opening in July, 1990

Frontage of the Bentall Centre in Clarence Street

Part of the atrium in the Bentall Centre

The Board of Bentalls in 1988, from left to right: David Fowler, Alastair Bentall, Grenville Peacock, Colin Popham, Edward Bentall, Andrew Noble, John Ryan and Tony Anstee and, behind them, a portrait of Leonard Bentall

Interior of the Bracknell store

Frontage of the Lakeside store

Part of the interior of the Tonbridge store

Statue of Leonard Bentall, 'The man who made Kingston', in the Bentall Centre

'Our Store, Your Store'   Chapter 5

Pat Moss, Mike Hawthorn (at the wheel) and Roy Salvadori taking part in Italy in Kingston

the Scottish Gathering of 1965 (deemed the most outstanding promotion of the year by the National Retail Merchants' Association of America) and Britain's Best at Bentalls in 1968 visited by HRH Princess Margaret, the same year in which Twiggy opened the new Just Now boutique.

Another important extension of the store was completed in 1964, the Fife Road extension, which like so many of its predecessors was attended by the latest in new technology – in this case a hot air curtain in place of doors, an air purifying system giving four changes of air an hour, high intensity lighting, a series of display 'gondolas' and counter units made by Remploy under licence from West Germany. From the customers' point of view, it marked the introduction of a degree of self service in that an increasing range of merchandise could be seen and

ITALIA ROMANTICA at Bentalls

Now on until Saturday May 9

Italy comes to Bentalls with all the excitement, warmth and atmosphere of this colourful country. See Italian craftsmen at work, taste Italian food and wines, listen to Italian music, enter a competition with holidays in Italy to be won, see Italian merchandise throughout the store—all this and more during 'Italia Romantica' at Bentalls.

KINGSTON UPON THAMES

OPEN UNTIL 7 P.M. FRIDAYS AND 5.30 P.M. SATURDAYS · CLOSED ALL DAY WEDNESDAYS

One of the posters for Italia Romantica

selected without having to wait for an assistant. There was also a self service restaurant, the Mulberry Tree, proclaimed as Europe's most modern store restaurant, as well as the waitress service Thames Room, the two replacing the old Tudor restaurant. The development was completed by the replanning of the 22,000 sq ft fashion floor with air conditioning and new fixtures which was opened by Mary Quant in 1970.

The company's centenary in 1967 offered an irresistible opportunity for a series of customer attractions though coinciding as it did with one of Harold Wilson's deflationary budgets it

'Our Store, Your Store'   Chapter 5

The replica of Michelangelo's David, complete with fig leaf to cover British sensibilities, outside the Kingston store

was more restrained than it would have been in more favourable economic circumstances. For all that it was a striking exhibition, with a reconstruction of Frank Bentall's original shop and adjoining premises, including the Clarence Arms which dispensed beer at the contemporary price of 1d per pint, though not for very long . . . Bentalls' long established suppliers ran concurrent displays highlighting their long association with the Kingston store. There was a boat trip to Greenwich for all those employees who had completed 25 years' service or more, and 150 took part. The exhibition was the occasion for another

Royal visit, this time HRH Princess Alexandra who lives in Richmond Park and was also a Bentalls customer.

One of the biggest bugbears for Kingston shoppers over the years since the war was the increasing difficulty of finding somewhere to park. Finding one morning in December 1968 every available car park filled by 11am, Rowan Bentall decided to act, first with a demand to the local council for more spaces, and secondly by commissioning a multi-storey car park for use by Bentalls customers and other shoppers as well, providing 750 parking places and costing £325,000. It was ready by the following November, a quite extraordinary achievement given the planning procedures, less complex than now it's true, and constructional obstacles to be overcome. It incorporated such innovative features as automatic control systems, numbered parking spaces, passenger lifts and – another feature in which it anticipated current legislation – spaces on the ground floor reserved for disabled drivers. The plaque, unveiled by the then Minister of Transport, read: BENTALLS MULTI-STOREY CAR PARK, AN ACHIEVEMENT FOR THE BENEFIT OF THOSE WHO USE THE ROYAL BOROUGH OF KINGSTON UPON THAMES AS THEIR SHOPPING CENTRE OFFICIALLY OPENED ON FRIDAY, 21ST NOVEMBER 1969 BY THE RT HON ERNEST MARPLES MP.

By 1971, nearly half a million cars a year were using the new facility. Other interesting statistics for that year were that 40,000 children had visited Father Christmas in the Bentalls grotto in the six weeks it was open; the store's export office was supplying customers in 85 different countries abroad; the estate office sold over 200 properties; and Bentalls were official outfitters to more than 100 schools. At this date the store had 150 departments retailing merchandise. Its range of additional services included:

'Our Store, Your Store' Chapter 5

The multi-storey car park shortly after its opening

- restaurants
- garage
- car sales
- removals and warehousing
- estate office
- post office
- insurance
- theatre tickets
- travel bureau
- furnishing consultants
- furnishing workrooms
- dispensary and opticians
- ladies', children's and men's hairdressing.

The same period was noteworthy for the introduction in Kingston of six day trading, the store opening all day on Wednesday, as well as for the introduction of decimalisation (on 15th February 1971) which as far as Bentalls were concerned was effected smoothly enough, much time and effort having been expended on making preparations for it, not to mention the cost of £120,000 for converting equipment.

Bentalls were more preoccupied at the time with what they saw as an unwelcome development, the birth of the out-of-town hypermarkets and superstores. There was a degree of self interest in their concern, to be sure, but they also foresaw the adverse effect such developments would have on town centres generally. Twenty-five years on and their concerns have been justified by events, resulting in the very recent removal of Government planning policy on the subject.

The company coped with the introduction of VAT in 1973 in much the same way as they had dealt with decimalisation two years earlier, making careful preparations and giving customers the benefit of any pricing adjustments wherever possible. For example, they eliminated halfpence from most prices by rounding them off downwards and either reduced or held prices at pre VAT levels.

The company and the customers suffered from the Government's emergency measures to restrict the use of electricity in the winter of 1973, coming as they did at the peak period of Christmas trading and making it necessary for Bentalls to close all its stores for two of the seven trading days prior to Christmas. The problem was exacerbated by the inevitably uneven pattern of delivery from manufacturers, Bentalls' answer to which was to increase stocks – involving additional high finance and increasing costs – to enable them to meet their customers' requirements with the minimum of delay. Efforts to control prices in support of Government anti inflationary policies put profit margins under further pressure. It prompted a *cri de coeur* about mounting pressures on private enterprise. 'The frustrations, the interference with legitimate trading and the opposition from many quarters to private enterprise today are severe,' wrote Rowan Bentall. 'Politically motivated taxation, soaring general rates and increasing legislation discriminate against the retail trade.' He went on to argue that the proposed Industry Bill with provisions for the disclosure of confidential information and extension of state ownership would damage the business life of the nation. 'Though taxed and legislated against from so many directions Bentalls are as determined as ever to stand up and fight for freedom of choice and enterprise and will not be deterred from giving to our wide and increasing circle of customers a service in shopping which is much appreciated and still quite unique with its personal touch and atmosphere. In doing so we shall also seek to give a satisfactory return to our stockholders on their investment, and security and proper reward to those employed in the organisation.'

Sales the following year received a considerable boost after the Government's decision to increase VAT to 25 per cent on radio, TV and electrical goods – and an inevitable slackening off once the increase was introduced. But another revolution in shopping habits was beginning with a sudden growth in the use of credit cards. Bentalls had resisted the move initially but in 1975 they began accepting Access and Barclaycard in addition to American Express and Diners and staged their first At Home evenings in the Kingston, Bracknell and Worthing stores for account customers, a tradition which continues to the present.

The next year, 1976, was the year of yet another spectacular promotion which was to give Bentalls a good deal of satisfaction in years to come.

It began with an approach from their near neighbours, Hawker Siddeley Aviation, to help inspire reciprocal trade with Finland. It resulted in 'Friendly Finland', which introduced a whole new range of stylish, high quality yet competitively priced furniture and other merchandise to Bentalls customers – and went some way to helping Hawkers, now British

Aerospace, secure aircraft orders worth £128-million, described in Chapter 3.

Later the same year Bentalls became the first department store in the county to win an award from the Council for the Disabled for the facilities provided at the Kingston and Bracknell stores.

In the meantime a major modernisation scheme for the ground floor of the Kingston store was being planned to enable Bentalls to meet the challenge of the 1980s. It entailed the installation of air conditioning, new lighting and the re-fixturing of a number of departments, the aim being to make the store one of the most attractive and up-to-date in the country, able to more than hold its own with any of its London competitors.

After years of deliberation, debate and delay, Kingston Council finally agreed on a new town plan in 1979 that was to pave the way for the rejuvenation of the town as arguably the best shopping centre in the South East outside London. It provided for a new traffic flow to alleviate the vehicular stagnation for which Kingston was developing a reputation (and which got progressively worse before it got better) with the arrival of the new one-way system in the town, coupled with the pedestrianisation of Clarence Street, in 1989. It also proposed the development of the Horsefair site opposite Bentalls for another large department store (developed, as it turned out, by the John Lewis Partnership) as well as the redevelopment of Bentalls' own site.

Edward Bentall, the present chairman and fourth generation of the family to become head of the business, assumed the chairmanship in 1982 on the retirement of James Spooner and the following year a range of strategic studies began, including most notably from their customers' point of view a review of merchandising policies to make sure they were geared to meet changes in the retail environment. This led to the highly successful and far reaching appointment as marketing consultants of the New York based Walter K Levy Associates Inc that was to have a profound effect on Bentalls' philosophy for the next decade. It was founded on a very thorough analysis of the needs and buying habits of Bentalls' customers, initially in the clothing sector of the business, which led in 1986 to a major revision of the company's buying policy and the refurbishment of the men's and women's clothing departments. It was augmented by a high profile advertising campaign based on the weekend colour supplements in the *Sunday Times* – the first time Bentalls had advertised nationally since the days of Leonard Bentall. They were created round the theme of 'The Bentalls Look and The Bentalls Style at Very OK Prices'. Another consequence of the Walter Levy marketing strategies was the increase in Bentalls' own-label merchandise, not only in clothing but in many other departments as well, and the introduction of lines exclusive to Bentalls. This in turn led to the gradual reduction in the number of concession shops by particular manufacturers within the store, which meant that more of the merchandise on offer was under Bentalls' direct control.

The disposal of the removal business in 1989 to some extent reflected the fact that it had been a difficult year for retailing and especially for the housing market and that the new store did not have as much space as the old for the marking and storing of goods. It was also in line with Bentalls' strategy to concentrate on the core business of retailing. Over the years the distinctively-shaped Bentalls removal vans had been a familiar sight throughout Surrey and further afield, and thousands of families had benefited from their efficient and ever courteous service. One bizarre event worth recalling occurred in the days of Leonard Bentall, when Bentalls were asked to quote for the removal of a house-load of furniture from

Kingston to a tiny island off the coast of France. The main obstacle was the lack of cranage on the island, which meant that items of any size had to be unloaded at a larger island nearby and transhipped by motor boat – time consuming, expensive and risk-prone. However, the removals department discovered after making typically thorough enquiries that a tramp steamer regularly carried stone quarried on the island to the UK. The owner readily agreed to transport a return cargo of furniture, which was lifted in crates by the ship's derricks directly on to the island's quayside. Bentalls' quote was 50 per cent lower than the next and all the furniture arrived in one piece.

In 1990 Kingston's shoppers were able to rejoice in the opening of the new Bentalls store as well as that of the new John Lewis store opposite shortly afterwards. With one of Marks & Spencer's larger branches only yards away, it created a unique shopping triangle. The opening of the Bentall Centre two years later meant that Kingston offered a range of opportunities to satisfy the most discriminating of shoppers, who began coming from an increasingly wide catchment area.

It happened not a moment too soon; as the recession began to bite in 1992, Bentalls and their fellow retailers needed all the help they could get.

6. *Branching Out*

THE BUILD-UP OF BRANCH STORES

Bentalls did not begin branching out geographically until after the Second World War, 80 years after the business was founded. Thereafter, branch stores have been added at the rate of one every decade. There are now five of them, one in Berkshire, one in London, one in Essex, one in Kent and one in Sussex. Two others, both in Kent, have now ceased trading. Most of the branches were bought as existing businesses, and most offered the possibility of enlargement or expansion. The principal exception was at Bracknell in Berkshire which Bentalls built from scratch in the then new town in 1973. The most recent of the branches, that at Thurrock in Essex, was added in 1991.

The advent of Bentalls' first store outside Kingston in 1947 was a family affair in every sense of the phrase, entailing as it did the acquisition of a store which had been opened by Frank Bentall's brother Charles in 1875, nearly 10 years after the former had established the Kingston store. It had been run by Charles and later by his three sons who were now wanting to retire and sell up. It was by accident, in the way of a chance remark, rather than by design that the Kingston family acquired the store, but it was an ideal arrangement for both parties, especially since the name continued more or less the same, as Bentalls (Worthing) Ltd instead of Bentall & Sons Ltd. Albeit much smaller than Bentalls in Kingston it was still a substantial enterprise, being in two sections, one fronting South Street and the other Liverpool Street, divided by a *cul de sac* but linked at first floor level by a covered bridge. By a happy coincidence the furniture department was designed by Sir Aston Webb & Sons, architects of the famous Bentalls frontage in Kingston. Not long after the change of ownership Bentalls succeeded in acquiring some adjoining shops and expanding the store. Further acquisitions and expansions followed in the late 1960s including the installation of escalators and the expansion of the nearby Portland Road warehouse.

Worthing Council suspended the half day closing requirement in the summer of 1971, the move proving so successful that, after a referendum, full six day trading was allowed throughout the year. It created an upsurge of trade for retailers in the town, not least Bentalls. The centenary of the expanded store – by now one of the leading stores in Sussex – was celebrated in 1975 with a series of special events.

There was some development in the late 1970s, when Bentalls built over a public road to form new departments (for haberdashery and knitting wool), coupled with the acquisition of the furniture and soft furnishing business of Jordan & Cook 30 yards away. This was used to accommodate Bentalls' furniture departments which in turn made space available for expanding the fashion floors and introducing a coffee bar, record department and ladies' hairdressing salon. It was followed by the acquisition of a 7,500 sq ft warehouse in Littlehampton to replace an earlier facility which the store had outgrown.

The hurricane which caused so much damage in the South East in 1987 ripped away sections of the roof of the Worthing store and paved the way for an extensive rebuilding programme and redecorated frontage as well as the installation of a new lighting scheme which served to highlight particular areas of merchandise. The trend towards increasing the number of Bentalls own ranges of merchandise in place of other manufacturers' concessions began to make an impact soon afterwards, particularly on the fashion floors but also in the men's department with a new range of carefully chosen men's shoes, as well as in the cutlery shop and with the arrival of a new tailoring department. In the nearby furniture building, which had always suffered from a difficulty of access to some of the floors, a new staircase was installed.

The 10-year development of the Bentall Centre in Kingston put something of a brake on further investment at Worthing and other branch stores during the 1980s but this changed at the end of 1993 when a comprehensive refurbishment of Worthing began. Two new escalators were installed and a new shopfront presented a more modern face to the world in the recently pedestrianised Montague Street precinct which the store overlooks. There were new ceilings, new lighting and new shopfittings throughout the ground floor, followed in the spring of 1995 with a new shopfront on South Street and new lighting and shopfittings on the upper floors.

The opening of Worthing branch was one of the first moves made by Gerald Bentall after succeeding his father, Leonard, as chairman. It was followed by that of a drapery business in Ealing three years later in 1950 for £250,000. Eldred Sayers & Son had been going since 1872 and had a modest return frontage of about 50ft on Springbridge Road. Only the ground floor of the premises had been developed to any great extent, hence there was scope for expansion. There were also a number of nearby shops with deep gardens behind, which in Bentalls' practised eyes were susceptible to offers, as proved to be the

The Worthing store following its face lift in the 1960s

case. For all that, the matter needed sensitive handling, since the future goodwill of the store was dependent on it, and agreement was reached with all the tenants concerned amicably enough. There remained, however, the problem of the old man and his dog to whom one of the tenants had sub let a small room behind a newsagent's shop. The man was 81 but in good health and hadn't the slightest notion of moving. Eventually, Bentalls were able to circumvent the impasse by buying him a small cottage nearby and allowing him to live rent free for the remainder of his days. The ghost of Leonard Bentall doubtless nodded his approval.

The Ealing branch has always been uniquely different from Bentalls' other stores by virtue of being so close to central London and hence, to all intents and purposes, a West End store. Customers' tastes are different and so are trading patterns, though some of the most significant differences have been political. The store comes under the authority of Ealing Borough and the Greater London councils whose ideas have often been at variance with those of smaller town and urban authorities. For example, whilst Bentalls and other retailers were enjoying the benefits of six day trading in Kingston and Worthing in the early 1970s, Ealing Council refused to hold a referendum on the subject despite a petition which Bentalls initiated. The Council finally relented towards the end of 1974. At the same time there was concern at the lack of parking spaces in the Borough, though this was alleviated by the opening of a 500 space multi storey car park just a few yards from the store in 1976. This encouraged Bentalls to invest in a number of improvements and innovations, with a new china and glass department including a Royal Doulton shop, modernised fashion floor and furniture and furnishing departments, enlarged coffee shop, reorganised food hall, new men's shop, shoe department and book department.

However, when the Ealing Broadway Centre was developed in the 1980s on the opposite side of the road, Bentalls decided to re-evaluate their Ealing situation. The development potential of the store was greater than its existing use, they reasoned, and so it would be wise to maximise this potential. Their architects drew up plans for an office development. In 1981, Bentalls submitted a planning application for the re-development of the Ealing store as a major office building with some 80,000 sq ft of lettable office accommodation and several small shops on the Broadway and Springbridge Road frontages. At the same time they entered into preliminary negotiations for space in the Ealing Central Development Scheme on the other side of the Broadway from the existing store. To the company's dismay, though the planning application was approved in principle by the London Borough of Ealing and recommended by the planning officers of the Greater London Council, the GLC itself turned it down. Bentalls duly appealed. The appeal was dismissed, on the grounds that the bulk of the building was too large for the site, though it was made clear that the site *was* suitable for redevelopment. A revised scheme was prepared

THE MEN WHO MADE KINGSTON

The original Ealing Store

and submitted for approval. Again it was approved by Ealing Council. Again it was turned down by the GLC. And again Bentalls appealed – having, in the meantime, entered into an agreement to lease the major unit in the re-named Ealing Broadway Centre, due to open for trading in September 1984. In the end, Bentalls sold the old store (with planning permission) for the sum of £4.3-million at the end of 1984. It was bought by Waterglade, the developers, who built a shopping mall which has proved something of a disappointment. Bentalls settled for cash rather than equity, a shrewd move in the event, and used it to fit out a new store in the Broadway Centre, opposite the Saunders department store, a small store in the old tradition. To Bentalls' advantage, a few years later the Saunders family sold up to Marks & Spencer, at once removing a competitor and adding a store which provided considerable drawing power to the area.

The store's position in the Broadway Centre is ideal, its principal entrance facing the main square and being adjacent to Marks & Spencer who opened there in 1991. The latter's arrival attracted new customers to the Centre and, because their trading pattern in Ealing was based on a 60-40 ratio of food to clothing, Bentalls' clothing and fashion accessories departments benefited. The Ealing premises cover some 46,500 square feet spread over two floors, making it the fourth largest of Bentalls' branch stores, with a staff of about 80.

Tunbridge Wells, the third of the branch stores, came into the Bentalls fold in 1960. Again, it was an exiting business. Again, it offered the possibility of expansion by means of the acquisition of adjoining premises. Founded in 1935, it was a fashion and accessory business trading under the name of Mary Lee and centrally located in the town's main shopping street. The range of merchandise was narrower than that offered by Bentalls and was confined to the upper end of the fashion trade. Efforts to broaden the appeal with the introduction of new departments and a coffee shop began paying dividends within a year or two of the change of ownership. The name remained unchanged until 1980, when it became Bentalls. But it continued to trade as a fashion store first and foremost because of its comparatively small size, its 16,000 sq ft of sales area making it the smallest in the group.

A modernisation to the store in 1987 which included one of the passenger lifts, hitherto one of the old-fashioned cage types which afforded views of the store through the bars as it moved up and down, proved too much for one customer. She declined the use of the new lift to take her to the hairdressing salon on the first floor and refused to walk up the stairs, insisting the stylist came down to her. Needless to say, Bentalls obliged.

The development of the Tunbridge Wells town centre over the past few years, with the opening of the Great Hall Precinct in the mid-'80s and the Victoria Shopping Development in 1992, bringing in Fenwick, an extension to Marks & Spencer, Woolworths, Boots and British Home Stores as well as increased car parking capacity, have all been to the benefit of the branch. Nevertheless, after a careful review of branch store operations, Bentalls came to the conclusion that the Tunbridge Wells store was too small to offer a sufficiently representative range of merchandise. The age and configuration of the building conspired against plans to upgrade it to a satisfactory standard, and so it was decided to cease trading there in the summer of 1995, staff being offered alternative employment in other branch stores.

Bentalls' fourth branch store, in Bracknell, was unique in being the first to have been purpose built for Bentalls. The decision to build it, taken in 1968, was made with an eye to benefiting from the planned expansion of what was then a small market town in Berkshire. Bracknell Development Corporation had begun building the new town in 1951 and its planned size had doubled in the meantime. But it lacked a department store, which its burgeoning population of young married couples with growing families were clearly going to need. Preliminary research showed that no fewer than 2,000 account customers from Berkshire were already using Bentalls' Kingston store; when it came to establishing their identity in the town, they already had a foot in the door. Geographically, being 20 miles to the west, it fitted the Bentalls' pattern of branch development and there was the advantage from the marketing point of view that it shared the same London evening newspaper and television network as Kingston. With their own experience in Kingston very much in mind, part of the agreement Bentalls reached with the Corporation was that there would be ample car parking not just near the store but actually linked to it; the fourth floor of the 1,000-car, nine level multi-storey park has a covered link bridge to the first floor of Bentalls. They ensured, furthermore, that the store development afforded scope for expansion and they also negotiated the availability of up to 30 moderately priced homes in the new town for staff purchase.

So far as the other branch stores were concerned, Bentalls had inherited a customer base when they acquired the premises. In Bracknell they were starting almost from scratch, and a great deal of effort during the construction period was devoted to establishing a profile of their prospective customers and their likely needs. Part of the effort took the form of evening talks open to the public and discussions with local women's and other organisations.

When it came to planning and equipping the new store, Bentalls' executives followed the company tradition of visiting recently built stores abroad – including North America, the Far East and Europe – as well as at home. Many of the ideas they came back with were incorporated in the new building, among them two notable 'firsts' for a European store. One was the latest range of point-of-sale computerised terminals, which, for the first time, recorded not only the price but details of the goods bought, forerunners of the type now commonplace at check-out tills all over. Another benefit the system provided for the customers was that they were able to collect goods from different parts of the store and pay for them at a single point. The pattern is familiar enough now, but at that time items purchased in one department had to paid for in that department. The second was an environmentally friendly (this in the mid '70s) heating and air conditioning system based on the principle of heat recovery. This draws out the air heated by store lighting and other equipment as well as that generated by the presence of customers, purifies it, then feeds it back into the store at a pre-controlled temperature. Features which had proved successful in the Kingston store were also incorporated, such as the warm air curtain at the entrance doors and the pram park.

The store opened in April 1973 and among the first visitors on opening day were Their Royal Highnesses Prince and Princess Richard of Gloucester. Reflecting its customer base, it was a young store in more senses than one, including the type and presentation of its merchandise and the youthfulness of the executives and staff led by 37-year-old David Fowler who had joined Bentalls' training scheme immediately after graduating from Oxford and later became a member of the Bentalls Board.

Ten years after the opening, a link was constructed between the store and the newly opened Princess Square Shopping Centre which proved a sound investment; within a year the store had increased its contribution to the group by 70 per cent. In effect it gave the store two ground floors, each with a main

The opening of the Bracknell store by HRH Prince and Princess Richard of Gloucester; Noel Anstee is on the left of the picture and Rowan Bentall on the right

entrance – the original one to the High Street and the new one to the shopping precinct.

With Bracknell poised to increase its population from 87,000 to 100,000 between 1985 and 1995, a major new scheme was on the stocks for an additional 180,000 sq ft of retail space together with extensive leisure facilities some 200 yards from Bentalls' store. The Skimpedhill Redevelopment opened in 1989, another bonus for Bentalls who had carried out a programme of improvements to the store in anticipation of the new business which resulted. With its 66,000 sq ft of sales space, making it the largest of the branch stores, the store has established itself in the eyes of the local Council as well as the shopping public as the premier store in the town.

Every business has its share of failures. For Bentalls the most conspicuous has been the branch store at Chatham in Kent. As with Worthing and Tunbridge Wells, it involved the acquisition of an existing business, one which was almost as old as Bentalls itself. The department store of Edward Bates Limited was established in 1869 and Bentalls acquired the whole of the issued share capital together with the adjoining premises in Chatham's High Street in August, 1978. The adjoining premises were vacant, having been occupied previously by a Sainsburys supermarket. Bentalls felt they could take on both halves of the building and create a successful if modestly sized (40,000 sq ft of sales and service area) town centre store.

One of the key problems was that it was at the northern – Rochester – end of the High Street, the opposite end to the Paragon Shopping Centre. Thus, the value of close proximity to shopping centres, so well demonstrated at Bracknell, was not available to them, though it *was* to a competitor, Allders, who opened a much larger store at the southern end of the High Street shortly after Bentalls' arrival. Another, more damaging, blow followed when Medway Council developed its relief road, a high level highway, which had the effect of isolating the store even more from the main shopping area.

The *coup de grace* came shortly afterwards with the announcement that Chatham Dockyard was to close. For centuries it had been one of the main sources of employment, directly and indirectly, in the Medway towns, giving rise to ropeworks, sailmakers, flagmakers and a host of other small industries. The effect of the closure on Chatham in particular was devastating, psychologically as well as practically, and retail sales were hit badly. To a store already making losses, the only one of Bentalls' branches to do so, it was the last straw. Early in 1984 the decision was taken to cease trading. Some local observers felt Bentalls should have hung on; others felt they were a shade up-market for the Kentish town where folk call a spade a spade. Perhaps they were right. Even Bentalls' departure had its frustrations. The incoming tenant at first agreed to take just half the building, hence the partition walls Bentalls had removed to extend the store had to be rebuilt. This done, the tenant decided to take the whole store after all. Down came the partitions once again . . .

In the same year that the ill-starred Chatham development got under way, Bentalls were embarking on another enterprise in a different part of Kent. This was a joint venture in Tonbridge with Sainsburys. It entailed the development of the former Kent county cricket ground into a supermarket linked to a department store with ample facilities for car parking. It was to prove a successful formula, with a high percentage of cross traffic between the two stores, located as they are within the Angel Centre shopping and leisure complex. The whole of the sales floor of the Bentalls store, which covers some 35,000 sq ft, or about twice the size of its neighbouring branch in Tunbridge Wells, is on ground level, with a coffee shop and hairdressing salon on the mezzanine floor.

In 1987, five years after opening, the store underwent a £175,000 refurbishment, prompted by faults in the expansion joints along the length and breadth of the ground floor. The need to re-floor and re-carpet provided a ready made opportunity for implementing the marketing concepts in ladies' fashions and menswear being developed for the Bentalls group of stores by the New York based Walter J Levy Associates. In addition, as part of a replanning of the merchandise layouts throughout the sales floor, the route from the common entrance between Bentalls and Sainsburys was redesigned to accommodate 'impulse' buys, whereas so-called 'planned' purchase items moved to another part of the store. The refurbishment took less than six months to complete and with careful planning was achieved without the loss of a single day's trade. It paved the way for a significant increase in sales in the years that followed.

In its 10th year the Tonbridge branch underwent an internal reorganisation which included a major planning of the menswear department, the expansion of the china and glass departments and the new departments for books and cutlery, coupled with the introduction of a home measuring service for furnishings. A 'high street enhancement scheme' was introduced by Tonbridge Borough Council in 1992 as a means of countering competition from new shopping facilities in Sevenoaks and Tunbridge Wells through pedestrianisation and improved facilities from which the store has benefited. More recently, work has been put in hand to increase car parking and customer access at the branch itself and it is hoped that the new arrangements will attract many of the loyal Bentalls customers from the Tunbridge Wells store following the decision to cease trading there in July 1995.

The record shows that since Worthing was acquired in 1947 Bentalls have opened a new branch store in every succeeding decade, more by accident than hard and fast design. The opening of the most recent addition, that at the Lakeside Shopping Centre in Thurrock, Essex, came in 1991, 10 years after Tonbridge. Like Bracknell and Tonbridge, it represented a plunge into what for Bentalls were uncharted waters. Here was a site in one of the new out-of-town shopping centres, next door to the M25 and close to the new Dartford bridge. Indeed, it was heralded as one of the biggest shopping complexes in Europe with 1.3-million square feet of sales area accommodating 300 retail outlets and parking for 9,000 cars. It was calculated that it was within one hour's drive of 20 per cent of the population of the United Kingdom. (The developers neglected to read their own publicity; not long after it had opened, would-be customers were driving away because they could find nowhere to park; an extra 3,000 spaces were added in 1993.)

The premises which Bentalls acquired in 1991 had been occupied at the time Lakeside opened the previous October by Lewis's Limited, the group which some months later went into receivership for reasons unrelated to the Thurrock store. They provide a sales area of 61,000 sq ft (some 5,000 sq ft less than Bracknell) on three floors, ideally located opposite Marks & Spencer, with Debenhams and House of Fraser nearby. Despite the brevity of the previous tenant's stay, the store required a complete refit as new departments were added – china, glass, housewares, household textiles, children's clothing, toys and a bookshop.

Coincidentally, the landlords at Lakeside with whom Bentalls negotiated the 35-year lease were among the prospective developers of the Bentall Centre in Kingston, Capital & Counties. The deal forged by Bentalls at Lakeside was an attractive one financially, the more so after Bentalls, on appeal, secured a 50 per cent reduction in the Uniform Business Rate. The outlook seemed promising, but trade at first was slow. Bentalls moved in before the opening of the Queen Elizabeth

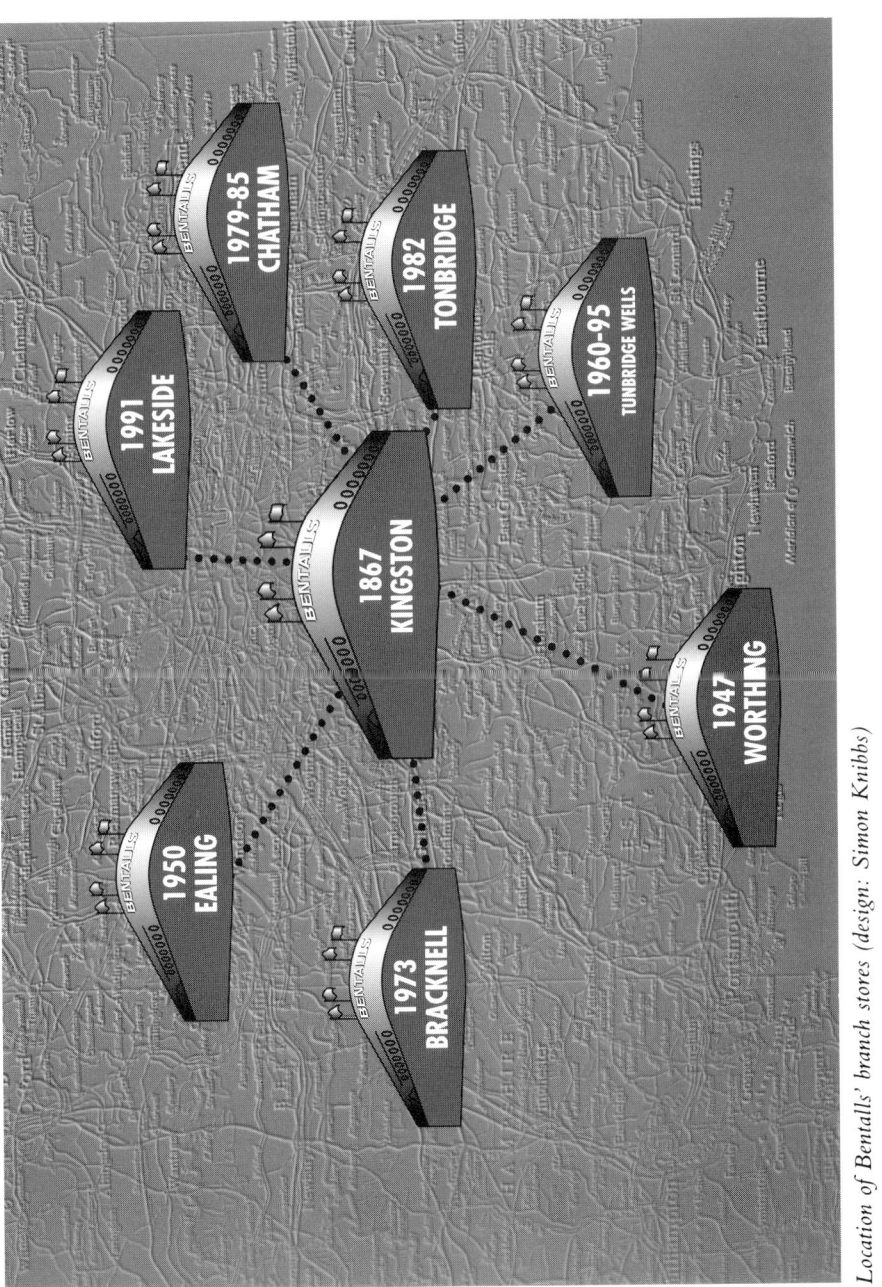

Location of Bentalls' branch stores (design: Simon Knibbs)

Bridge when traffic delays at the notorious Dartford Tunnel were frustratingly frequent. Bentalls the department store group, unlike the Bentalls of agricultural machinery fame, were unknown in Essex. Nor were Bentalls familiar with the tastes of so-called Essex Man nor (more significantly in their merchandising mix) Essex Woman and they soon realised they had much to learn about their tastes. They were quick to do so, modifying their merchandising and their advertising to cater for a market that has its idiosyncrasies (just as those stores in Surrey, Sussex, Berkshire, Kent and London have theirs), introducing longer opening hours and different staffing arrangements. Lakeside, for example, has two general managers whereas all the other Bentalls stores have only one. By the autumn of 1994 the store had begun to trade profitably.

7. 'The Planning Application of the Century' – I

THE GRADUAL ACCUMULATION OF LAND AND PROPERTY

The Bentall story is a remarkable one in many respects – the stature and vision of Leonard Bentall, the character of the Bentall family across four generations, the flair and courage shown in innovation. Yet in some ways the most remarkable of all is the way in which it has developed into a 600,000 sq ft store and shopping centre on the very same site as Frank Bentall's original shop. The process of acquisition, which took the best part of a century and a quarter to complete, is at once one of patience, speculation, inspiration, determination and some good fortune.

A look at the plan on pages 138–9 shows how the various pieces of this intricate jigsaw slotted into place. The site is rectangular. Clarence Street, now Kingston's main shopping street, forms the shorter southern side of the square, Wood Street forms the western and – turning right as it does towards Kingston Station – the northern side, and Fife Road the eastern. A short distance to the west of Clarence Street is

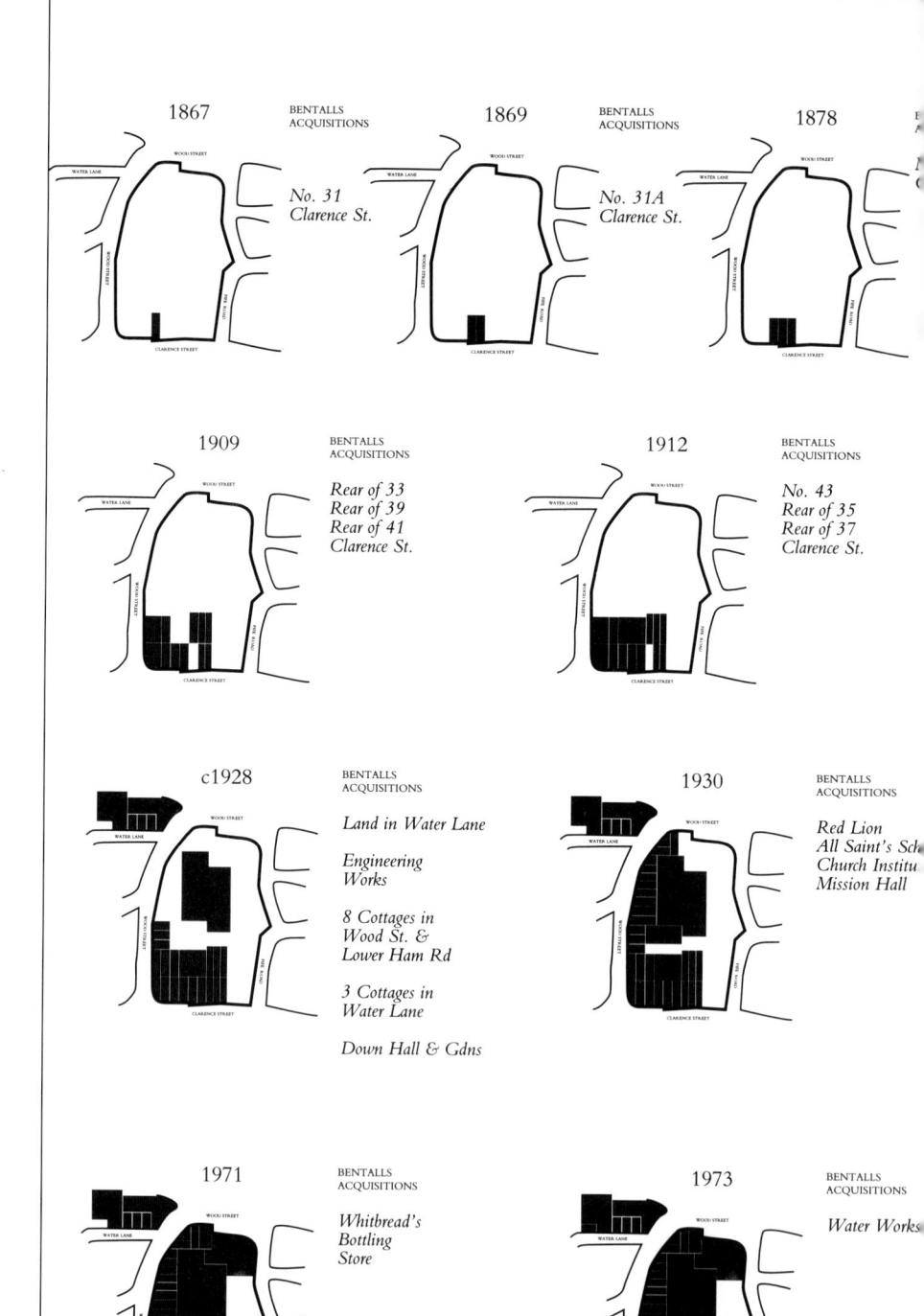

1867	**BENTALLS ACQUISITIONS** *No. 31 Clarence St.*	**1869**	**BENTALLS ACQUISITIONS** *No. 31A Clarence St.*

1878

1909	**BENTALLS ACQUISITIONS** *Rear of 33* *Rear of 39* *Rear of 41* *Clarence St.*	**1912**	**BENTALLS ACQUISITIONS** *No. 43* *Rear of 35* *Rear of 37* *Clarence St.*

c1928	**BENTALLS ACQUISITIONS** *Land in Water Lane* *Engineering Works* *8 Cottages in Wood St. & Lower Ham Rd* *3 Cottages in Water Lane* *Down Hall & Gdns*	**1930**	**BENTALLS ACQUISITIONS** *Red Lion* *All Saint's Sch* *Church Institu* *Mission Hall*

1971	**BENTALLS ACQUISITIONS** *Whitbread's Bottling Store*	**1973**	**BENTALLS ACQUISITIONS** *Water Works*

1900	BENTALLS ACQUISITIONS	1902	BENTALLS ACQUISITIONS	1906	BENTALLS ACQUISITIONS
	Nos. 25 & 27 Clarence St.		*Rear of 25 Rear of 27 Clarence St.*		*Nos. 39 & 41 Clarence St.*

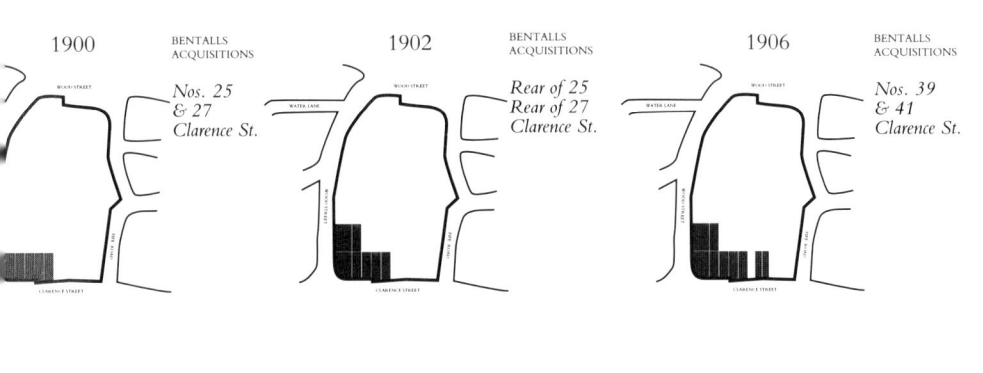

early 1919	BENTALLS ACQUISITIONS	late 1919	BENTALLS ACQUISITIONS
	Clarence Arms Nos. 10, 12 & 14 Wood St.		*Nos. 16, 18 & 20 Wood St. Vicarage & Vicarage garden (1½ acres)*

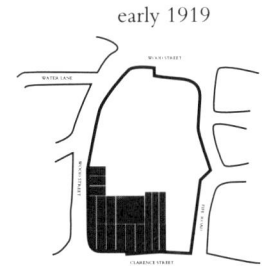

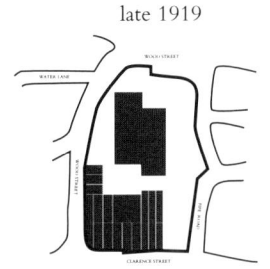

1934	BENTALLS ACQUISITIONS	1957	BENTALLS ACQUISITIONS
	White's Factory *Cottages* *Railway Tavern*		*Fred Ide & Sons*

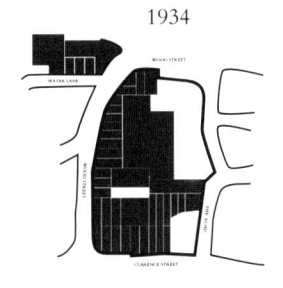

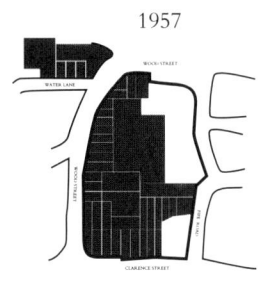

1987	BENTALLS ACQUISITIONS
	Snooker Hall *Outfitters* *Wire Works*

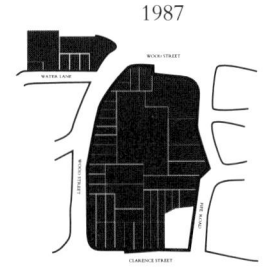

↑ N

Plans (not to scale) of the site in Kingston showing Bentalls' acquisitions of land and property since 1867 (design: Simon Knibbs)

Kingston Bridge. Kingston Parish Church is on the southern side of Clarence Street, immediately opposite the south west corner of the Bentalls site. To the south of the Parish Church is the old Apple Market.

When Frank Bentall acquired Clarence House in 1867 the Market was the focal point of the town and Clarence Street was on the fringe, with only farm fields beyond. Clarence House, No 31, was in the middle of Clarence Street and the earliest property acquisitions were to the west in the direction of the river, save for No 31A, the yard adjoining Clarence House, which Frank Bentall acquired and covered in. At first it was not a rapid process by any means. The shop next door on the river side, No 29, was not acquired until 1878; Nos 27 and 25 did not follow until the turn of the century, the land to the rear of them being added in 1902. However this had taken Bentalls to the end of Clarence Street to the corner with Wood Street. The next move was in the opposite direction. Next to No 31 was the Clarence Arms which was to remain a public house for the next 20 years. But beyond that were several more shops, Nos 35 to 43, towards the Fife Road corner. By now the pace of growth had begun to quicken, stimulated by the increasing influence in the business of Frank's younger son Leonard. It was he who had the vision to negotiate the purchase of a piece of land running from the rear of the Clarence Arms to the rear of No 41 with a right of way through to Fife Road. It was a crucial move in the context of the department store that was still to come, since it enabled Bentalls to link up with their shops at the other end of Clarence Street.

Properties to the east of the Clarence Arms were acquired over the next few years, Nos 39 and 41 in 1906 and Nos 35, 37 and 43 in 1912. It meant that when in 1919 the Clarence Arms finally succumbed, the Bentalls enterprise occupied a continuous stretch along the Clarence Street frontage and the area

'The Planning Application of the Century' – I   Chapter 7

Wood Street in 1886

immediately behind it. It was, in the true sense of the phrase, a landmark achievement, and its conclusion may well have satisfied a man of less vision than Leonard Bentall. He, though, had already set his sights in the direction of Wood Street.

At that time, Wood Street was no more than a narrow lane, a mere 15 feet wide. Leonard's initial acquisitions caused more than one eyebrow to be raised. In his booklet *The Rise of Bentalls* describing the company's first 80 years, Herbert Perkins, Bentalls' first company secretary, wrote: 'When in a discussion I ventured to suggest that this property was hardly worth purchasing as the thoroughfare was absolutely dead from a business point of view, I well remember Mr Leonard quoting Emerson: *If a man can write a better book, preach a better sermon or make a better mousetrap than his neighbour, though he build his house in the woods, the world will make a beaten path to his door*, and adding: 'If you live long enough, you will see in Wood Street one of the finest buildings in the county and the road one of the best

141

in the town.' Well, it was then only a vision, but the man behind it had the will, energy and foresight to make it come true.'

He'd begun by buying three small properties in Wood Street (Nos 10, 12 and 14) but in 1919, the year in which the Clarence Arms was acquired, he purchased two more (Nos 16 and 18) in addition to the vicarage and, significantly, the 1½ acre vicarage garden. It was a great *coup* since it permitted a very considerable expansion of the store northwards along Wood Street. Several obstacles remained, not least the Red Lion pub on the Clarence Street/Wood Street corner, but this in turn was acquired in 1930, in addition to All Saints' School, the Mission Hall and the Church Institute. It gave Bentalls a substantial 'L' shaped landholding of approximately two thirds of the present site.

Four years later, the store's expansion on the eastern, Fife Road, side was effected through the acquisition of White's Mineral Water factory, together with a row of cottages and the Railway Tavern in Ceres Road, the road running parallel with the railway along the northern boundary of the site which is now an extension of Wood Street.

Aside from the main site, Bentalls had bought other properties during the same period, including residential accommodation to house members of staff. But the most important of all were opposite the north west corner of the site where Bentalls' multi-storey car parks now stand. This was in the 1920s, and as well as cottages, land and a small engineering works, they included Down Hall, a country house the grounds of which extended as far as the river. It provided the space Leonard needed for his car park and restaurants, which became the talk of the 'thirties, as well as land enough to build new headquarters for the Steadfast Sea Cadet Corps.

Long after Leonard's dream of a superstore had materialised there were some further acquisitions without which the Bentall

Centre of today, occupying as it does 4½ acres, would not have been possible. In 1957, the premises occupied by Fred Ide and Sons in Fife Road were purchased. Ides were traditional ironmongers and occupied fairly substantial premises where the Fife Road entrance to Bentalls is now situated and as part of the deal they were rehoused on the opposite side of the road. In 1971, Whitbread's bottling store in Wood Street was acquired. This was a significant addition because it was a large building and occupied a strategic position at the north east corner of the site. Its acquisition virtually completed the rectangle. It had taken just over a century, but the site as we know it today was all of a piece. A year or two later, across the road to the rear of the multi-storey car park, Bentalls made another important acquisition, the premises of the Water Board between Water Lane and Vicarage Road. Its importance may not have been fully appreciated at the time but it was to facilitate the vital one-way system at the rear of the Bentall Centre car parks.

Even more vital once the Bentall Centre plan was on the drawing board was the need for a service road to serve the store and the Centre. It posed a problem. Of the obvious candidates, Clarence Street was due to be pedestrianised and both Wood Street and Fife Road were busy main roads. There was a narrow access road beside the former Whitbread bottling store in the north east corner of the site and although it connected with Wood Street it stopped some way short of the proposed Fife Road entrance. In the way were a wire works, a gents' outfitters, the Dolphin public house and a snooker hall. The first three were acquired without too much difficulty, albeit at a price. The fourth remained obdurate and by now the indispensability of the service road to Bentalls' plans was well-known. Bentalls already owned the freehold of the snooker hall and so were legally entitled to buy back the lease but at the same time they were obliged to pay the tenants compensation. One of a pair of independently owned snooker halls, the other being in Hatton Garden off Holborn Circus, the premises were very popular and from time to time attracted celebrities of the calibre of Ray Reardon. On that account alone the amount of compensation sought was substantial but the figure was inflated by Bentalls' desperation to push the road through. In the end they settled for a sum considered to be well over the odds. Nevertheless, the last obstacle had been removed, the link road between Wood Street and Fife Road could be built, and the scene was at last set for a development that might have caused even Leonard Bentall to raise an admiring eyebrow.

'The planning application of the century' – II

THE CONCEPT AND DEVELOPMENT OF THE BENTALL CENTRE

In the late 1960s and '70s, Kingston's traffic problems were becoming acute. Roads were saturated with traffic. Parking was all but impossible and on Saturdays Clarence Street was impassable, despite a one-way system introduced in the '50s which was never wholly successful and served only as a placebo. One of the root causes was the fact that more than 50 per cent of the traffic passing through the town was doing just that – passing through, from and to other destinations.

One of the consequences of the traffic problem was an inevitable falling off in trade that affected retail outlets throughout the town. Bentalls were among the most vociferous of those calling for action. But they acted as well, building a multi-storey car park for over 600 vehicles opposite the store which was opened at the end of 1969. It was a boon to thousands of shoppers. But it was not the answer to the main problem – the urgent need to improve the access roads.

Kingston Council decided that the answer was to build a relief road, the primary objective of which was to take traffic out of Clarence Street and Market Place and make both into a traffic free zone. Another priority was to open up views of the river by diverting traffic away from the riverside and opening up walks instead. A number of alternative schemes were put forward, the consideration of which took up a good deal of time.

Again, Bentalls were actively involved. In 1974 they instructed their architects, Elsom Pack & Roberts, to investigate the traffic problem with Kingston Council particularly with a view to the further development of their own site. The site was at the heart of most of the ring road schemes under discussion and, for obvious reasons, Bentalls were anxious to safeguard their own interests. In January, 1976, Rowan Bentall and his colleagues on the board invited representatives of the GLC, Kingston Corporation and their own advisors to meet to discuss proposals put forward for the replanning of the centre of Kingston and in particular the large open space opposite Bentalls' frontage in Wood Street known as the Horsefair. Another meeting followed in September, at which Bentalls raised doubts about several aspects of the proposals.

They were particularly concerned about a proposal to reduce the width of Wood Street, one of the store's prime frontages, and the fact that the proposals failed to make provision for increased numbers of cars coming into – and parking in – the town. Rowan Bentall argued: 'Only by an increased parking provision and an extensive development of the road plan to deal with the through traffic can Kingston hope to improve its reputation and position as a major strategic shopping centre in the future and make the increased shopping facilities a viable proposition.'

It was to take another two years before the new road plan was finally agreed. But as well as facilitating the flow of through traffic, it called for the pedestrianisation of Clarence Street (to

'The planning application of the century' – II   Chapter 7

Bentalls' obvious benefit) and allowed the development of the Horsefair site for another large department store (the John Lewis Partnership, as it was to turn out) six years hence. Bentalls welcomed the proposals, at the same time urging the Council to be mindful of the need for additional car parking facilities which at that time fell considerably below accepted levels.

With the road plan in place, Bentalls were free to consider the future of the store site and they began studying redevelopment plans. Among the options considered were a supermarket, an office block, an hotel and (the one which found most favour with the town planners) a new shopping mall with two multiple stores and several single unit shops and an enlarged multi-storey car park. During the next five years the plans were revised and reconsidered several times by the Bentalls board, now chaired by Edward Bentall, until agreement was finally reached on a proposal for developing the entire site. On 26 February, 1986, Bentalls announced the appointment of Norwich Union as developers of what was to be deemed by Kingston Council when it finally gave the scheme its blessing, 'the planning application of the century'. To quote from the Bentalls announcement at the time:

'The development will be known as The Bentall Centre and will be one of Europe's most exciting shopping centres incorporating the most modern design features. It will consist of a new Bentalls department store and approximately 100 new shops.

'The Bentall Centre will consist of four levels built around large central atrium with a glazed roof. It will have the characteristics of a new covered town square attractively laid out with seating and plants, making extensive use of marble flooring, mirrored walls and many specimen trees.

'Glass wall climber lifts and escalators will provide a central feature of the development. The store's existing Aston Webb

147

THE MEN WHO MADE KINGSTON

The Aston Webb Facade c1960

façade will be retained and integrated with the new Centre.

'The Centre will have a comprehensive retail mix within 260,000 square feet of new units available for leading multiples and speciality retailers. In addition, a food court will be constructed consisting of a variety of speciality restaurants situated round an attractive central seating area.

'The new store, which will have a gross area of 350,000 square feet, will trade on all four levels with direct access to the shopping centre at each level, and will therefore act as an anchor for the Centre. It will have a similar retail mix to the present Bentalls store but its modern purpose built design will enable merchandise to be displayed more attractively and efficiently.

'The present car park will be extended from the existing 620 spaces to bring the total number of parking spaces to over 1,200. A covered bridge will be constructed over Wood Street to link the car park with the new Bentall Centre.

'The proposed development complies with the principles laid down in the Kingston Town Plan but is still subject both to planning permission being obtained and to contract. It is envisaged that a detailed contract will be entered into before the end of 1986 and that development work will start in the first quarter of 1987. The new Bentalls store should be completed by the end of 1989 and the rest of the development during 1992.'

The building plan was one thing. The deal which Bentalls negotiated with Norwich Union was something else. The bones of it were that Bentalls would retain the freehold of the entire site, granting Norwich Union a 130 year lease. Norwich Union would bear the entire cost of the development, then estimated at some £110-million. They would also lease back the department store to Bentalls at a peppercorn rent. Furthermore – and in many ways this was to prove highly significant – Bentalls were to receive 23.59 per cent of the rental income from the retail shops in the development subject to a guaranteed *minimum* of £1.6-million annually. To say the least, the deal was highly satisfactory from Bentalls' point of view and perceived by the City as such. It was also a matter of some gratification to the board and to finance director John Ryan in particular – especially when, as the cold wind of the recession was blowing through the doors of the nation's shops, they had the warm comfort of a guaranteed rental income of £1.6-million each year coming in.

Planning permission was granted at the beginning of 1987, Kingston Council's director of planning remarking that a singular feature of the application was that its supporters far outweighed its objectors. There had been some modifications to the original proposal, increasing the cost of the scheme to £130-million and extending the timetable by a few months.

The link between the store and the offices/car park – an enclosed, steel bridge over 100ft in length – caused a ripple of excitement when it was installed. Fabricated near Stuttgart, it travelled by barge down the Rhine through Germany, was transhipped in Holland aboard a seagoing vessel to the Port of Tilbury in Essex, and transhipped again to a river barge for the final leg of the journey up the Thames to Turks Boatyard near Kingston Bridge. There it was offloaded on to road transport and taken up Water Lane to Wood Street where cranes were waiting to lift it into position.

The offices were the first part of the new development to be completed. Anstee House, as it was named (after Rowan Bentall's cousin and board colleague Noel Anstee), was occupied in May, 1990. Three months later the second part was opened – the new Bentalls department store, the largest department store to be built in the UK from scratch for over half a century. In the best Bentalls' tradition, the transition from old store to new was achieved smoothly in the space of 72 hours on a hot humid July weekend. The old store closed on Saturday – fittingly enough with a Blue Cross sale – and the new one opened on Wednesday, 25 July, following a special preview evening for chargecard customers. They'd begun queueing in warm sunshine during the afternoon; by the end of the evening, no fewer than 10,500 had been inside the new store.

An outside observer, writing in the *Bentalls Bulletin*, the group's staff magazine, described the new store thus:

'Spectacular is the word that quite literally describes the new Kingston store. Its sheer spaciousness is the first thing to strike the visitor – that and its 'user-friendliness'. Although its overall area is smaller than that of the store that it replaces, it is so well planned and laid out that it actually appears to be larger; and in fact it has the largest sales area of any department store to be built in the UK since the war.

'The most dramatic feature is the massive central atrium through which, as if in perpetual motion, move 13 flights of escalators. They afford incomparable views of every floor; it is possible to 'window shop' with the greatest of ease throughout almost the entire store simply by riding from one floor to the next.

'En route, the things which most readily attract the senses are:

- The geometric patterns, sharp edges and bright colours giving a classically modern look from top to bottom;
- The colours and perfumes of the dried flowers which seem to rise up from the well of the lower ground floor;
- The polished bronze *art deco* clock at the head of the lift shaft;
- The two glass-enclosed, wall-climber lifts which themselves afford superb views of the interior of the store;
- The illuminated stained glass in the ceilings at each entrance dating back to the 1930s and preserved from the original store;
- The natural light flooding in through the atrium roof and the photosensitive lighting system, which in response to the external light, gradually brightens or dims accordingly;
- The two smart new restaurants – the Atrium Cafe (table service) on the first floor and the Bentalls Brasserie (self-service) on the second;
- The Continental styled delicatessen and wine store;
- The Wolsey Hall Exhibition area.

'Even as he leaves, the visitor is in for another visual surprise as he walks across the high level, glass encased walkway straddling Wood Street, past the stylish new management offices – now self-contained in a separate building immediately opposite but readily accessible to the new store – to the *two* car parks providing space for 1,200 cars all told. And, for the not-so-regular visitor to Kingston, there is yet another pleasant surprise – the new and vastly improved one way traffic system which has transformed the approaches to and from the new Bentalls.'

Customers interviewed for the same publication were no less enthusiastic for the most part, though some older customers (several of whom had been shopping at Bentalls for over 50 years) had some regrets at the passing of the old store. A Glasgow woman thought it all a little brash but with characteristic logic concluded: 'Bentalls have always offered me good value for money, so I'll keep coming, despite the decor!' But a woman from Roehampton who'd lived most of her life in the USA 'loved' the new store and was pleased to see that 'at last, we're catching up with the American stores'. A man who had written to Bentalls in 1964 to praise the courteous service of a young sales assistant was delighted to meet the same person, now a marketing director, on his first visit to what he called 'an absolutely magnificent building'. A lady who had not been to Kingston for 30 years travelled in from Wiltshire for the opening and pronounced it 'absolutely mind-blowing'. But it was the young lady from Chessington who had the last word: 'It's a beautiful place. It just makes me want to spend money . . .'

Two years later, in November 1992, the huge Bentall Centre redevelopment was completed, appropriately enough in Bentalls' 125th anniversary year. The event had a royal prelude the previous August when Her Majesty the Queen unveiled a plaque to mark the restoration of the famous façade in Wood Street by Sir Aston Webb (the architect who designed the frontage to Buckingham Palace) which had been retained as part of the redevelopment. But with the recession putting a damper on trade and a brake on the speed with which the 100 retail units in the 600,000 sq ft development were being let, the Centre opening was a lower key affair than otherwise might have been the case. Nevertheless there were some big names

'The planning application of the century' – II   Chapter 7

in place for the big day, among them W H Smith, Dillons, HMV and Disney, and within a year nearly 50 per cent of the units had been let and were trading. Eighteen months later, some 86 per cent of the retail space was trading, or in the course of fitting out, or in the final stages of completion. By the autumn of 1995, approximately 95 per cent of the space had been let and the roll call of retailers in the Bentall Centre read as follows:

Allsports	Early Learning	Oakland Menswear
Aroma Secrets	Ecco	Paco Sweaters
Austin Reed	Esprit	Promod
Bay Trading	Faith	Pumpkin
Bella Ricco	Five to Twelve	Rodier
Bentalls	Fosters	Sock Shop
Blakes	Game	Sofa Workshop
Body Shop	Gap Kids	Spoils
Boots Health & Beauty	Golfland	Starlog
	HMV	Suits You
British Airways	Index	Talbots
Circa	Intersport	TGI Fridays
Ciro Citterio	Jeffrey Rogers	The Pier
Clinton Cards	Jerry's Home Store	The Stencil Store
Cookie Jar	Jewellery Store	Tie Rack
Crabtree & Evelyn	La Senza	Torq
Cromwells Mad House	Levi's	Toystack
	Mark One	Vision Express
David Clulow	Mothercare	W H Smith
Dillons	NatWest Bank	Warner Bros
Disney Store	Natural World	Wax Lyrical
Dunn & Co	Nordic Sport	Whittards

It was quite an achievement during a time of inactivity in the shops and office property sector and begs the question whether, if the development had not been finalised before the recession, it would have gone ahead at all. Almost certainly

153

the Bentalls of the recession-ridden 1990s would have had the courage of the Bentalls of the depression-driven 1930s. Whether they would have found a financial backer is another question.

In retrospect, the Bentall Centre development was driven by three key considerations. The first was to take advantage of the long-awaited relief road scheme, without which it certainly would not have been possible to attract retailers to the Centre, let alone a developer. The second was the threat that if Bentalls failed to redevelop their site, a predator would come along and do it for them. The third, and most decisive, was the recognition by the Bentalls board that the site that had been built up gradually by the patient endeavours of their predecessors had very considerable potential waiting to be unlocked – for the future benefit of the shareholders, the company and their customers.

8. A Store for All Seasons

THE FAMILY INFLUENCE AND THE MANAGEMENT OF BENTALLS

For all but four of the 128 years of Bentalls' existence the company has been headed by a Bentall. Frank, the founder, brought in his two sons, George and Leonard, in 1889 and 1893 respectively so that when he retired in 1909 they were well placed to succeed him. By that time the business had grown from a single shop into a small department store with some of the features that were to characterise it in later years, including its fleet of vans, tea rooms, electrical gadgetry and mail order. Leonard Bentall, the driving influence behind many of these innovations, was to be its guiding star for the next 30 years; he more than any other individual was responsible for its development into a department store to rival any in the land.

His brother George retired in 1917, leaving Leonard in sole control. He had the support of loyal and enthusiastic senior managers and in order to free himself of certain responsibilities, he appointed two of them, Maurice Harcourt and Herbert Perkins, as joint managers. Maurice Harcourt was the general manager and had been with the company over 20 years. Herbert

Perkins had joined Bentalls from Harrods as mail order and publicity manager. In 1925, two years after the death of Frank Bentall, Leonard decided to convert the business into a private limited company and both became directors. W Astles, who had joined in 1911 and was then merchandise manager, became the third. The fourth was Leonard's elder son, Gerald, just 22 years of age and three years in the business. Leonard's younger son, Rowan, joined his father and elder brother in 1930 after a year's training with Harrods and became a director six years later in the same year as R J Machin and a year before Eric Fleming.

Gerald was appointed general manager at the age of 25 and had been managing director for several years before Leonard's death in 1942. He therefore became his natural successor, Rowan becoming merchandise director. The brothers took up the reins during the difficult post war years. They had inherited a remarkable business, but with it an unenviable overdraft of £500,000 and a legacy of £300,000 in death duties.

The short term solution to the financial problems was to go public, which they did on 8 November 1946, offering 200,000

Gerald C Bentall *L E Rowan Bentall*

two shilling shares at 30 shillings each. This represented a 25 per cent stake in the business, the other 75 per cent remaining in the Bentall family. It is interesting to reflect that fewer than 100 UK companies listed at that time are still in existence. Coincidentally, ICI also went to the market in 1946 as did MEPC, one of the developers in competition for the Bentall Centre, just five days before Bentalls.

The longer term solution was the continuing expansion of the business. Within a year of the decision to become a public company, they began to develop in a completely new direction. Hitherto, all Bentalls' acquisitions had been confined to the Kingston area, driven mainly by the desire to expand the store on the same site and also to provide service and staff facilities nearby. But in 1947 it was learned that a store in Worthing which had been founded by Frank Bentall's brother Charles in 1875 was for sale. It was a perfect opportunity. The second cousins were amenable. The Bentalls name would be perpetuated. The price was agreed. The concept of branch stores had been established and was to grow with each succeeding decade.

Back at the Kingston store, Rowan's influence began to make itself felt in the increasing number of special promotions being staged, the younger son having inherited his father's flair in this respect. But his sphere of activities was more widespread and he became deputy chairman in 1950 and in due course succeeded his brother to the chairmanship.

In the intervening period the board took a significant and in those days rather exceptional step. In 1953 it appointed the Hon William, later Lord, Mabane as a non-executive director. If Bentalls were looking for outside expertise they could hardly have picked a better man. MP for Huddersfield, assistant Postmaster-General then successively secretary to the ministries of Home Security and Food during the wartime Coalition government, he ran his own substantial shoe business and was also a director of Kemsley Newspapers, proprietor of *The Times* and *Sunday Times*, for whom he wrote articles on taxation. He had influence with opinion formers in the right places; it was no accident, for example, that the person who opened the re-built car park in 1969 was the former Minister of Transport, Ernest Marples. Lord Mabane served on the Bentalls board for 12 years, during which time he became chairman and later president of the British Travel Association.

A year after William Mabane's appointment, Noel Anstee joined the board. He was a cousin of Gerald and Rowan. His father, John Anstee, was a civil engineer from Guildford who married Leonard's sister Mabel in 1906. When Gerald suffered a heart attack in 1963, Rowan and Noel Anstee became joint managing directors. Between them they pursued a policy of increasing Bentalls' land holding on the Kingston site, buying properties adjacent to the store as they became available, including most notably the acquisition of the Whitbread brewery site which now forms the entrance to the new Kingston store. Without their foresight it is questionable whether the recent Bentall Centre development would have been possible.

Bentalls celebrated their centenary in 1967 and one of the ways in which they did so was to commission a company coat of arms. The Bentalls having been an armigerous family since the 1500s, they had had their own coat of arms and motto, *servabo fidem*, 'I will serve with faith'.

The new company coat of arms, with the motto 'To strive, to seek, to serve', is based on that of the family but has one or two important differences. Instead of the coronet on the former, the latter has a haberdasher's hat, and the leopard which stands above the hat sports a flying scarf in the Bentalls' house colours of green and cream. The shield of the company coat of arms incorporates a salmon representing the Royal Borough of Kingston and its proximity to the River Thames where in Saxon times there was a thriving salmon fishery.

Gerald retired in 1968, to be succeeded as chairman by Rowan, who was to hold that office for the next 10 years. These were buoyant times, profits reaching a record £1-million in 1969, having doubled in the space of a decade. The following year Bentalls were among the 500 largest quoted companies in the UK and were rated the 13th largest store in Europe. Soon afterwards, Rowan began working on a history of the first hundred years of the company. There had been a biography of Leonard Bentall, *A Merchant Adventurer*, written by Charles Herbert and published in 1936, and several historical booklets, notably *The Rise of Bentalls* written by Herbert Perkins covering the years 1867 to 1951. Rowan's book, *My Store of Memories*, was much more ambitious in scope and detail; published in hardback in 1974, it was reprinted in 1980, 1988 and 1992. In his introduction he explains its *raison d'être*, which dated back to a book signing in the store by the comedian Ted Ray in 1972: 'Like Ted Ray I have a fondness for recalling the past so afterwards, over a well-earned lunch, it was natural that we should swap stories of his friends in the entertainment world who had been attractions at the store during the Thirties – people such as Sydney Jerome and his famous band and Petula Clark who made one of her earliest appearances as a child singer, standing on a chair and being paid with a bag of sweets. From there I went on to recount other tales of the store, large and small, which I had accumulated over the 40-odd years in the family firm; the day of the great potato queue, the curious affair of the unsellable soup, the night the bomb hit the piano department, the man who stopped the runaway horse, and many more.

'A fellow guest then asked me why I had never set down these stories, and I had to reply that although I had always wanted to do so, the time never seemed ripe. Hearing this, my eldest son, Edward, insisted that the time had now arrived, pointing out that many of the fascinating stories of the store's formative years would be lost for ever if they were not recorded quickly. This was only too true; already many stalwarts of my father's day had passed on and other Bentall pensioners, with a personal knowledge sometimes stretching back for 50 years, were getting that much older. It was now or never, so to speak.'

In 1973, six years into Rowan's chairmanship, another non-executive director was appointed. William Semple had just relinquished his appointment as chairman and chief executive of Army & Navy Stores. A self-made accountant and an Ulsterman, he'd joined Army & Navy as a boy and worked his way up to become managing director, then chairman. He had a penchant for property development through which he had transformed his own company's fortunes. In him, Bentalls saw the ideal successor to Rowan, who planned to retire in 1978 and whose eldest son, Edward, was still in his 30s and not yet ready to take over. William Semple was due to become vice-chairman within a year of his appointment of non-executive director. But in the meantime, two senior managers from Army & Navy had joined Bentalls. The move was seen as the beginning of a mass defection in the direction of Kingston. House of Fraser, who by then had acquired Army & Navy, took strong exception. There was a heated disagreement between House of Fraser and Bentalls. The outcome was the resignation of William Semple.

Bentalls were more fortunate in their next non-executive appointment, that of James, later Sir James Spooner. He joined them in 1976, became deputy chairman in 1977 and succeeded Rowan as chairman in 1978. The only non-Bentall to hold the chairmanship, James Spooner was at the time chairman of

James Spooner *Edward Bentall*

NAAFI and of the Spirella Group as well as being deputy chairman of Hogg Robinson and the National Mutual Life Assurance Society. He therefore brought considerable experience and a wide ranging knowledge to the post. But he did much more than serve as an able chairman and bridge the family gap for four years. Subtly but significantly he changed part of the nature of Bentalls.

Until 'Mr' Rowan's retirement, everyone on the board, even though they had served on it for 20 years, called one another by their surnames. With James Spooner came first names and a less formal style of dealing with colleagues and with staff. He had another trait which, at first, went against the Bentalls grain. At the end of every board meeting he stood up, tore his board papers in half and tossed them into the wastepaper basket. Rowan, who filed *everything* and had, not one but two, separate offices for the purpose, was horrified. In time he came to accept, even to laugh about it – secure in the knowledge that *his* papers were intact.

The succession had been astutely planned. On James Spooner's appointment as deputy chairman, Edward Bentall,

Rowan's eldest son, had been made joint managing director with his father. Edward, a chartered accountant, had joined Bentalls in the finance department soon after qualifying in 1964 at the age of 25, and had been appointed to the board in 1972. When Rowan retired from the chairmanship in 1978 and was appointed Bentalls' first president, Edward assumed the full responsibilities of managing director. When James Spooner retired four years later, he became the fourth generation of Bentalls to head the family business his great grandfather had founded.

His chairmanship has coincided with a time of profound change in the department store business coupled with some significant shifts in the economic climate in the UK. Increasing competition and differences in buying habits over the past 15 years have created problems for retailers in general and department stores in particular of the kind with which his predecessors would have been unfamiliar. They have called for moves as radical as any introduced by Rowan, Gerald, Frank or even Leonard Bentall. One such move was the decision to redevelop Bentalls' most priceless asset, the four and a half acre site built up by a gradual series of calculated acquisitions spanning more than a century. It was a decision of immense significance and one which the Bentalls board debated over a number of years. Had it not been taken at the time and in the way that it was, it is debatable whether Bentalls would have been able to continue trading in the way that they have. As it is, the decision to redevelop the site has given Bentalls a brand new department store tailored to the needs of the future as well as a guaranteed rental income from the remainder of the site, the freehold of which Bentalls retain.

The second significant move was to take a completely fresh look at the needs and tastes of their customers and to adapt their merchandise accordingly. The change has been gradual, necessarily so since Bentalls have been anxious to avoid alienating the thousands of customers whose loyalty to the 'old' Bentalls has been one of the great strengths of the business. But it has been revolutionary nonetheless and has seen the emphasis shift to give more focus to fashion for the family and for the home. As part of the change, store layouts at Kingston and all the branches have been altered fundamentally to enable departments selling related merchandise to be located adjacent to one another. The change has also seen the disappearance of many of the 'concessions' (shops within a shop) that were a feature of the previous store but which conspired to give the impression of Bentalls as a high priced store. They have been replaced by a high percentage of Bentalls' own-brand merchandise in many different areas. As the 'OK prices' slogan of the 1990s indicates, Bentalls have been at pains to dispel that impression.

Gone, possibly for ever, are the days of departmental stores which conformed with Leonard Bentall's ideal of providing everything that man, woman and child might need to clothe and feed them and furnish their home. The 'offering' nowadays, whilst still extensive and highly competitive, is narrower and more reflective of the changed buying habits of the customers.

It was during the development of the new store and the associated Bentall Centre that Bentalls weathered their first and so far only take over attempt. They had invited five leading retail property developers to tender for the development. Bentalls had written the rule book on how the tenders were to be presented and the financial structure of the bids. All five would have incurred substantial costs in putting together their teams of architects, surveyors, design consultants, letting agents, and so on, and in presenting their bids, hence the competition was keen. Following consideration of the initial presentations, Bentalls decided on a short list of two, Capital & Counties and Norwich Union. Detailed discussions with each followed, during which Capital & Counties proposed a grandiose plan which far exceeded the parameters of the Bentall Centre development and which also called for a much longer timescale – one of the reasons why Bentalls rejected it and settled on Norwich Union as their development partner.

Predictably perhaps, given the circumstances, Capital & Counties made an offer for Bentalls shares, allying themselves with an offshoot of the Bentalls family having a shareholding of about 5 per cent. The offer – it was never formalised into a bid and never likely to succeed – was eventually allowed to drop, though it caused a certain amount of acrimony and received coverage on Channel 4 Television's business programme. In the event, Norwich Union acquired the 5 per cent shareholding which they still hold and, ironically, the company with which Bentalls subsequently negotiated the lease of their newest store, that at the Lakeside shopping complex in Thurrock, Essex, was Capital & Counties.

Under Edward Bentall's chairmanship, the present board is a comparatively small one, consisting of three executive directors and three non-executive directors. The three former are Grenville Peacock, chief executive, who joined Bentalls in 1974 as general manager of the flagship Kingston store, having trained at Harrods and subsequently joining the Army & Navy division of the House of Fraser Group; John Ryan, finance and property director and company secretary, who joined Bentalls in 1983 from Ellerman Lines, having been financial controller of Ellerman Travel; and Tony Anstee, son of Noel Anstee and a great-grandson of Frank Bentall, who has been with the company since 1964 and whose role is that of services director. The three non-executive directors are Alastair Bentall, Edward's middle brother (the youngest, Piers, is general manager of the Worthing branch store), who joined Bentalls in 1963; Andrew Noble, a member of the board since 1987, previously managing director of store operations at Debenhams plc, and currently chairman of the Liverpool Victoria Friendly Society; and Michael Pickard, a non-executive director since 1993, formerly chief executive of Sears plc (of which Selfridges is a part) and currently chairman of the London Docklands Development Corporation.

Two other former non-executive directors made significant contributions during their time on the board. Denis Greensmith MBE, former managing director of Lewis's and Selfridges and on the board of Sears Holdings, served from 1981 until 1987 and brought with him a wealth of expertise in marketing. Colin Popham, former deputy chairman and managing director of the Bowater Corporation PLC, came in 1982 following the personal recommendation of Michael Morse of Capel Cure & Myers, and retired 10 years later, having in the meantime introduced to the board the successful concept of 'away days' to plan and develop their corporate strategy.

Most of the present board were closely involved in the 10-year-long development of the Bentall Centre from the very outset in the mid 1980s. All were engaged in steering the organisation through the debilitating recession which began having its effect on high street spending in 1990, two years before the Bentall Centre was completed. The parallel with the other comparable development in Bentalls history, the building of the new Kingston store in the 1930s, is striking. The essential difference between them is that the earlier store was conceived *during* the depression whilst the present one was planned during the buoyant 1980s. Its timing was fortuitous in two respects. Had it been delayed more than a year or two, it is hard to believe there would have been financiers courageous enough to provide funds once the recession had taken hold. As it was, the guaranteed rentals from the Centre once it was completed helped in no small measure to tide Bentalls over one of the most testing periods in its history.

*The Men
Who Made
Kingston*

Frank Bentall
Chairman 1867 to 1909

Leonard Bentall
Chairman 1909 to 1942

Gerald Bentall
Chairman 1942 to 1968

Rowan Bentall
Chairman 1968 to 1978
President 1978 to 1993

James Spooner
Chairman 1978 to 1982

Edward Bentall
Chairman 1982–

Index

Abershaw, Jerry 34
All Saints' School, Kingston 142
Allders 131
Anstee
 John 158
 Mabel née Bentall 158
 Noel 150, 158, 164
 Tony 164
Anstee House 150
Apple Market 140, 146
Archbishop of Canterbury 28, 32
Army & Navy Stores 160, 164
Astles, W 29, 156
Aston Webb façade 36, 51, 98, 147
Atrium Café 151
Attenborough, Sir David 57

Bedser, Alec 54
Bedser, Eric 54
Benetala, Anfrid de 5
Bentall
 Alastair 164
 Alice 16
 Anthony 6
 Charles 121, 157
 Edward 4, 34, 43, 59, 68, 84, 118, 147, 160–162, 164
 Frank 2, 5–10, 12, 14, 16, 18, 21, 26, 29, 52, 65, 71, 72, 87, 89–91, 103, 113, 121, 137, 140, 155–157, 162, 164
 George 16, 21, 28, 155
 Gerald 29, 76, 80, 81, 103, 123, 156, 158, 159, 162
 Josiah 5
 Laura, née Downman 5, 7, 14, 16, 21
 Leonard 3, 4, 16, 19, 21–32, 34–43, 45, 47, 49, 57, 69, 72, 73, 75, 77, 78, 79–81, 89, 91, 93, 99, 100, 102–104, 119, 123, 124, 137, 140, 141, 142, 144, 155, 156, 159, 162, 163
 Mabel 16
 Mrs Gerald 76
 Piers 164
 Rowan 2, 19, 47, 52, 54, 55, 57, 59, 62, 64, 69, 76, 79, 81, 83, 84, 86, 101, 103–105, 108–110, 114, 116, 146, 150, 156–162
Bentall Centre 3, 4, 36, 37, 51, 62, 85, 98, 120, 123, 134, 142, 143, 145, 147, 148, 152–154, 157, 158, 163–166
Bentall Hurricane Fund 80
Bentalls Brasserie 151
Bentalls Bulletin 85, 86, 150
Bentalls Sports & Social Club 81, 84
Bentalls Stores
 Bracknell 103, 117, 118, 121, 128, 129–131, 134
 Chatham 103, 131, 132
 Ealing 81, 103, 123–125, 127
 Kingston 2, 23, 24, 29, 30, 35–40, 42, 51, 54, 60, 117, 118, 125, 150–152
 Lakeside 103, 121, 134, 136
 Tonbridge 103, 132–134
 Tunbridge Wells 103, 127, 128, 131–133
 Worthing 76, 81, 103, 117, 122, 123, 125, 131, 133, 157, 165
Benthall Hall, Shropshire 5
Benthall, William 5
Bexhill-on-Sea 73

Bliss, Tom 101
Bloomingdales 103
Boots 128
Boyd-Carpenter, John MP 110
Bracknell Development Corporation 128
Braid, James 43
British Aerospace 117
British Army Museum 53
British Home Stores 128
Brooke, Mrs Barbara 107
Buckingham Palace 152
Bushey Park 53

Calvert, Phyllis 110
Cambell, Sir Malcolm 99
Capel Cure & Myers 165
Capital & Counties 134, 164
Car Park 32, 34, 35, 92, 114, 142, 143, 145, 148, 151
Carter, Howard 45
Cawthra, Hermon 32, 92
Ceres Road, Kingston 142
Chandler, Sir Colin 63, 64
Channel 4 Television 164
Chanut, Ferdinand 93
Charterhouse School 105
Chatham Dockyard 132
Chelsea Barracks 53
Chessington Zoo 101
Christies (Auctioneers) 2, 45
Christmas Circus 53, 100
Claremont Landscape Gardens, Esher 59
Clarence Arms 9, 24, 28, 91, 113, 140, 142
Clarence House 77, 140
Clarence House Members' Club 72
Clarence House Operatic Society 77
Clarence Street 7, 9, 10, 12, 16, 19, 21, 22, 24, 28, 35, 52, 65, 89, 91, 92, 118, 137, 140, 142, 143, 145, 146
Clarence, Duchess of 10, 65
Clarencia 72
Clark, Petula 159
Coldstream Guards 39, 45
Collins, Joan 56, 57
Coronation Stone 62
Council for the Disabled 118
Crane, Howard 35
Cromwell Road, Kingston 40
Customers
 profile 87, 119, 162
 relations 14, 23, 25–28, 30–32, 34, 35, 37–39, 71, 82, 87–89, 99, 116, 118, 133, 163

D-Day Remembered Exhibition 53
da Vinci, Leonardo 110
Daily Express 110
Daily Telegraph 110
Debenhams 103, 134, 165
Digby, Cllr F C 49, 69
Dillons 153
Dinky Toys 2
Disney 153
Dolphin (PH) 9, 10, 143
Domingo, Placido 57
Down Hall 34, 142

168

Index

Duke & Duchess of Norfolk 108
Dysart School 60

Ealing Borough Council 124–126
Ealing Broadway Centre 125–127
Edward Bates Limited 131
Eldred Sayers & Son 123
Electricity 2, 29–32, 37, 116
Elizabeth Fitzroy Homes 57
Elsom Pack & Roberts 146
Emerson, Ralph Waldo 141
English Heritage 69
Escalator Hall 96, 99, 101
Escalators 37, 38, 96

Fairfield Road, Kingston 72
Fife Road 38, 52, 62, 96, 111, 137, 140, 142–144
Fleming, Eric 99, 103, 156
Food Hall 96
Forest House, Woodford 22
Forte, Charles Lord 110
Fowler, David 57, 130
Fowler, Mrs Susanna 52
Fraser, Sir Malcolm 49
Fred Ide & Sons 143
Furniture Depository 34, 40, 42, 51, 60, 92

Gamages, department store 39, 99
Gibbon, Edward 2
Great Potato Sale 26–28, 159
Greater London Council 124–126, 146
Greensmith, Denis MBE 165
Guildhall 62

Hall, Messrs J E 37
Hampton Court Palace 3, 36, 60, 62, 98, 107
Hampton Court Park 67
Harcourt, Maurice 28, 29, 155
Harrods 25, 156, 164
Hatt, James 7, 10, 12, 87
Hawker Siddeley 62, 63, 80, 117
Hawthorn, Mike 110
Heath, Sir Edward 57
Herbert, Charles 159
HMV 153
Hockridge, Edmund 109
Honour, Derek 53
Horsefair 10, 118, 146, 147
House of Fraser 134, 160, 164

ICI 157
Innes, Hammond 105

Jarvis, Peter 59
Jerome, Sydney 159
John Lewis Partnership 118, 120, 147
John Mowlem 62
Jordan & Cook 122

King Athelstan 32
King Charles 34
King George VI 43
King Henry VIII 32
King John 32
Kingston 7, 8, 10, 12, 16, 19, 32, 36, 51, 60, 68, 118, 120, 146, 151, 152
  arts trust 59
  bridge 10, 32, 64–69, 140
  Chamber of Trade 66
  charter 32
  Corporation 9, 29, 31, 65, 100, 146
  Council 10, 11, 30, 59, 66–68, 118, 145–147, 149
  county court 35
  Gas Company 9
  Grammar School 2, 34, 57, 93

hospital 59
Parish Church 8, 9, 57, 108, 110, 140
railway 10, 12
regatta 59, 72
RFC 59
station 10, 137
vicarage 9, 19, 28, 32, 37, 142
Kittner, Anita 54, 101, 102
Knapp, Stefan 60, 61

Ladybird Books 2
Lamont, Rt Hon Norman MP 68
Lamson Tube Company 25, 28, 90, 92
Land acquisitions 2, 3, 18, 19, 24, 26, 28, 35, 40
Laver, James 60
Lewis's Limited 134, 165
Leyland, Maurice 54
Lidbury, Sir Charles 47
Lloyd George, Rt Hon David MP 100
Lord Howard of Effingham 8

Mabane, William Lord 157
Machin, R J 156
Macys 103
Mail order 25, 90
Maldon, Essex 5, 6
Mankowitz, Wolf 105
Mannequin Hall 54, 96
Marks & Spencer 120, 126–128, 134
Marples, Rt Hon Ernest MP 114, 158
Marshall Field 103, 106
Mary Lee 127
May, Peter 105
Medway Council 131
Merchant Adventurer 159
Metropolitan Police 105
Michelangelo 110
Middleton, C H 99
Minoprio 66
Moorish Tea Room 28, 91
Morse, Michael 165
Mulberry Tree Restaurant 112
Museum of Richmond 53
My Store of Memories 19, 52, 55, 86, 101, 159

National Trust 59
New College, Eastbourne 22
New Victoria Hospital 57
Noble, Andrew 165
Normandie Restaurant 108
Norris, Steven MP 68
Norwich Union 62, 147, 149, 164
Novello, Ivor 99

Occupational Health Department 75
Old Bentallians' Association 81

Packeteria 96
Palace Road, Kingston 73
Peacock, Grenville 164
Penrhyn Road, Kingston 40
Perkins, Herbert 25, 28, 29, 141, 155, 159
Peter Jones, department store 16
Peters, Sylvia 108
Pickard, Michael 165
Popham, Colin 165
Pram Park 38, 96
Prince and Princess Richard of Gloucester 130
Princess Alexandra 53, 59, 114
Princess Alice 42
Princess Helena Victoria 43
Princess Margaret 111
Professional Golfers' Association 60
Purley & Addington Schools 41, 73

169

THE MEN WHO MADE KINGSTON

Quant, Mary 112
Queen Adelaide 10
Queen Anne Boleyn 32
Queen Elizabeth I 32, 34
Queen Elizabeth II 62, 106, 152
Queen Mary 107
Queen Victoria 9

Railway Tavern 142
Ray, Ted 159
Reardon, Ray 144
Red Lion (PH) 9, 142
Reid Dick, Sir William 49
Removals Department 40, 119, 120
Richard, Sir Cliff 57
Richmond 67
Richmond Park 104, 114
Richmond Park Golf Course 43
River Thames 34, 36, 62, 66, 150, 159
Roberts Marine Mansion 42, 73
Royal Academy 32, 40
Royal Artillery 79
Royal Doulton 125
Royal Mail 35
Royal Russell School Society 42
Royal Welsh Fusiliers 47
Ryan, John 149, 164

Sadlers Wells 32
Sainsburys 131–133
Saks 103
Salvadori, Roy 110
Saunders, department store 126
Sears plc 165
Sears Roebuck 103
Selfridges 165
Semple, William 160
Sesame doors 28, 91
Slade School of Art 60, 61
South East Veteran Car Club 54
Special Promotions 2, 23, 32
  All British Show 25, 91, 104
  American Fair 110
  Blue Cross Day 90, 150
  Cricket fortnights 54
  Crime prevention exhibition 105
  Friendly Finland 2, 64, 117
  Hollywood Fair 102
  Italia Romantica 64, 110
  Italy in Kingston 64, 109
  Jimminy Jingle 106
  June Bride 108
  Nylon exhibition 105, 106
  Radio-Bentalls 39, 98
  Red Letter Week 90
  Scottish Gathering 111
  We Believe in England 104
Spirella Group 161

Spooner, Sir James 160–162
St Blaize 8
Staff
  numbers 18, 22, 36, 38, 51, 72, 76, 86, 102
  relations 14, 23, 26, 41, 71–77, 82–86, 142
  restaurant 82
  training 81, 84
Steadfast Sea Cadet Corps 34, 42, 57, 100, 142
Streatham Park 22
Strong, L A G 105
Sunday Times 119, 158
Surbiton 11, 12, 22
Surrey Comet 12, 28, 91

Tapper 41, 42
Tate, Maurice 54
Taylor, J H 43
Telford, Thomas 65
Territorial Army Bentalls' Battalion 77–79
Thames Room Restaurant 34, 112
The Times 158
Thornycroft, Mrs Peter 110
Tonbridge Borough Council 133
Tudor Restaurant 32, 34, 37, 54, 92, 112
Turks Boatyard 150
Tutankhamun 45
Twiggy 111

Vardon, Harry 43, 44
Vicarage Road, Kingston 143
Vickers 63

W H Smith 153
Walter K Levy Associates 119, 133
Warehousemen, Clerks' and Drapers' Schools 41, 42, 73
Water Lane, Kingston 143, 150
Waterglade 126
Webb, Maurice 36, 37, 40, 93
Webb, Sir Aston 3, 36, 42, 93, 122, 152
Westminster Bank 47
Whitbread 143, 158
White's Mineral Water factory 38, 142
Wilson, Harold Lord 112
Wimbledon Common 34
Wolsey Hall 54, 151
Wood Street 9, 10, 19, 28, 32, 34, 35, 37, 52, 62, 89, 93, 96, 137, 140–144, 146, 148, 150–152
Woolworths 128
World War I 26, 41, 78
World War II 53, 76–79, 102
Worthing Council 122
Wren, Sir Christopher 36
Wright Brothers 29
Wyatt, Sir Thomas 32

YMCA 43, 57

Zoppi, Count Vittorio 110

Detail of a design by Eric Gill for the Aston Webb façade of the Bentalls store in Kingston upon Thames

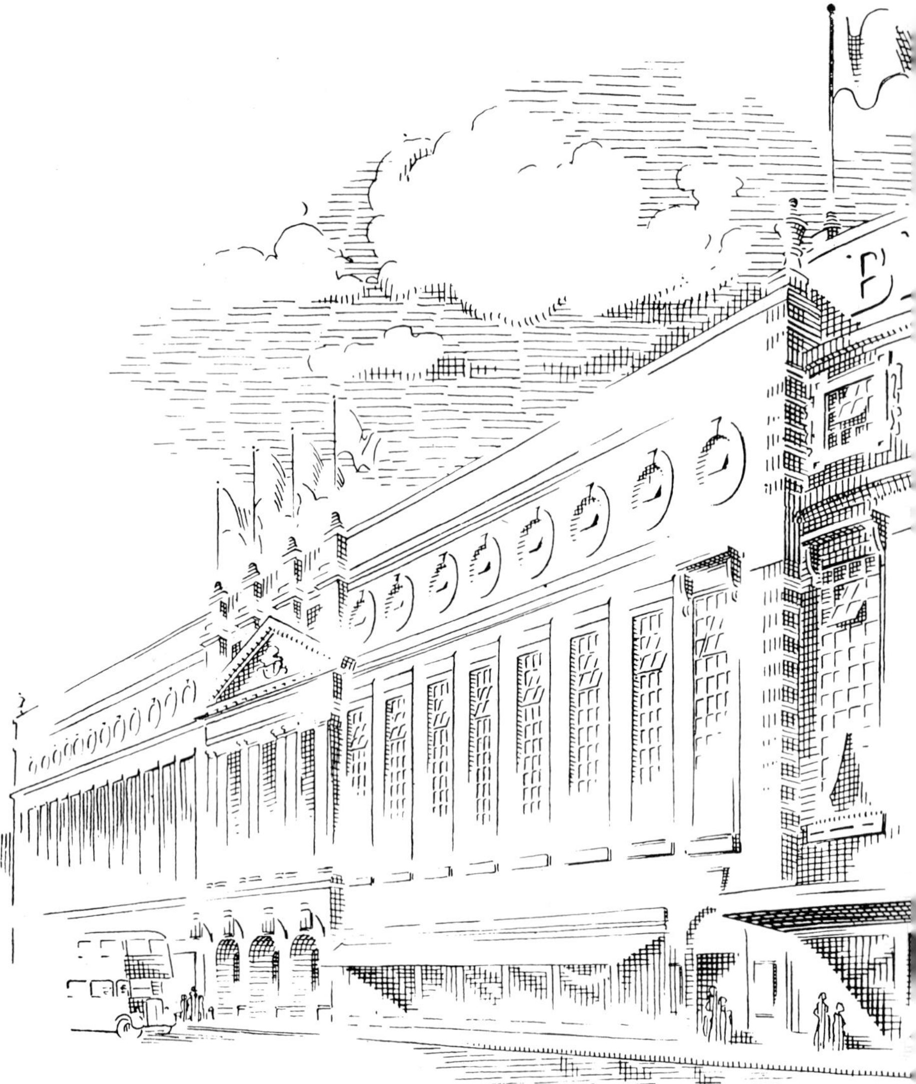